PAYING FOR HEALTHCARE AND OTHER FINANCIAL CONSIDERATIONS

Laura Town, Karen Kassel, and Sam Clapp

Silver Hills Press
Zionsville, IN 46077

ISBN: 978-1-943414-06-2

Production Credits:
Authors: Laura Town, Karen Kassel, and Sam Clapp
Publisher: Silver Hills Press
Photos: All images used under license from Shutterstock.com

Social Media Connections:
Laura Town
Twitter: @laurawtown
LinkedIn: http://www.linkedin.com/in/lauratown
GooglePlus: http://plus.google.com/u/0/117415714202281042310/posts
Pinterest: http://www.pinterest.com/laurat0428

Karen Kassel
Twitter: @KarenKassel1
LinkedIn: http://www.linkedin.com/pub/karen-kassel/62/2b/915/

Sam Clapp
LinkedIn: http://www.linkedin.com/pub/sam-clapp/48/549/554

TABLE OF CONTENTS

PAYING FOR HEALTHCARE AND OTHER FINANCIAL CONSIDERATIONS

Alzheimer's disease is an expensive medical condition, and managing the financial impact of the disease can be confusing and overwhelming. Alzheimer's disease is a double-edged financial sword: Your loved one's medical and care costs will be mounting as their capacity to manage their own finances is declining. Many caregivers struggle with the dual responsibility of managing their loved one's finances while also navigating the complex task of finding appropriate care.

The best thing my (Laura's) dad ever did financially was purchase long-term care insurance before he had any health issues. His policy covered the cost of his care for the six years he suffered with Alzheimer's disease, and that care was expensive! Home healthcare for Dad was around $9,000 per month, and that did not include medicine or food. Then Dad transitioned to assisted living, which, at $5,000 per month, was less expensive than home care but still cost more than most workers earn in a month. Dad next was placed in a memory care unit, which cost $7,000 per month. Neither the assisted living costs nor the nursing home costs included the prices of Dad's medications, which were as much as $1,000 per month when he was in the Medicare prescription "donut hole."

Costs for home healthcare and long-term care facilities are expensive, and the costs continue to rise each year. However, they are not the only costs associated with Alzheimer's disease. Care costs can range from a few dollars for home safety improvements to thousands of dollars per month for long-term individual care. The information in this book will provide more details on the costs of care you can expect as well as the resources available to help pay for these care costs.

Possible Costs of Alzheimer's Care

Caring for a loved one with Alzheimer's disease is extremely expensive. The average annual cost of healthcare and long-term care services for people with Alzheimer's disease and other dementias is around $46,669, and that figure does not include uncompensated caregiver costs or the general cost of living. In addition, this average includes individuals from mild-stage to severe-stage Alzheimer's disease. Typically, care costs will be lower in the mild stages and will progressively increase as your loved one needs greater care and supervision. Therefore, you need to know what to expect and what resources are available to you and your loved one to help pay for adequate care.

Care costs for a person with Alzheimer's disease are split into two categories: medical expenses and non-medical expenses. Different resources are available to help pay for each category of care. Medical expenses are usually paid by insurance, such as private health insurance, long-term care insurance, Medicare, or Medicaid. Non-medical expenses are usually paid using personal funds. Also, remember that the cost of caring for other medical conditions—for example, heart disease, cancer, or diabetes—will add to the cost of Alzheimer's disease care. Care costs vary by region, and medical costs will vary depending on the type of insurance coverage your loved one has. However, many individuals with Alzheimer's disease will face the same types of expenses, detailed in the checklists below.

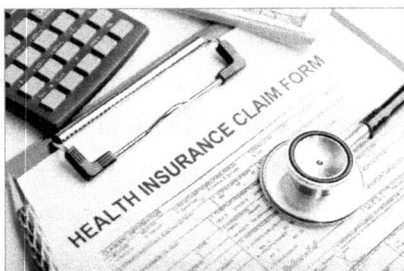

Checklist: Medical expenses

- ☐ Doctors' visits (including specialists)

- ☐ Laboratory/diagnostic tests

- ☐ Hospital stays (including psychiatric hospitals)

- ☐ Medical procedures

- ☐ Medical equipment (e.g., walker or cane)

- ☐ Therapy (physical, occupational, speech)

- ☐ Prescription medications

- ☐ Personal care supplies (e.g., for incontinence)

- ☐ Insurance premiums

Checklist: Living expenses

- ☐ Adult day care (approximately $60–$150 per day)

- ☐ Medical home healthcare (approximately $15–$25 per hour)

- ☐ Assisted living (approximately $35–$165 per day)

- ☐ Full-time residential care services/long-term care (approximately $115–$275 per day)

Checklist: Non-medical expenses

- ☐ Basic costs of living

- ☐ Increased costs for activities your loved one used to do on their own (e.g., home or vehicle maintenance, lawn care, driving, cooking)

- ☐ Home services (e.g., homemaker, companion, and/or personal care services)

- ☐ Home safety modifications

- ☐ Child care costs for individuals with minor or disabled children

- ☐ Emergency alert system

- ☐ Financial protection tools (e.g., identity theft protection, different phone number or post office box to help avoid scams)

- ☐ Taxes and fees associated with transferring wealth

- ☐ Attorney fees for creating legal documents or mediating court proceedings

- ☐ Counseling costs for the individual with Alzheimer's disease as well as caregivers, family, and friends

- ☐ Mediation costs for families with conflict

Most individuals or families cannot afford these costs from their own personal assets and must rely on other resources to help pay for care. However, knowing what options are available to help pay for care can seem overwhelming when the bills start pouring in. The next section details many resources and options that can help relieve some of the financial burden of Alzheimer's disease.

How to Pay for Care

The best way to help manage healthcare costs associated with Alzheimer's disease is to have quality health insurance and long-term care insurance policies. However, your loved one will likely not be eligible for long-term care insurance if the policy is not already in place when they are diagnosed with Alzheimer's disease, and a new health insurance policy may not cover Alzheimer's disease because it would be classified as a pre-existing condition. Without these insurance policies, your loved one will have to spend down almost all of their assets before they are eligible for Medicaid. To prevent this from happening, the checklists in this book will guide you through your loved one's financial options when paying for care, from private assets and insurance policies to public programs like Social Security, Medicaid, and Medicare.

Insurance Benefits

The costs of care for an individual with Alzheimer's disease will seem insurmountable without adequate insurance. Many individuals will have a private health insurance policy to help pay for healthcare costs. If your loved one is still working, this policy may be available through their employer, or they may have an individual policy. If they must quit their job after diagnosis, they will likely be eligible for COBRA insurance. If your loved one is retired, they likely have health insurance through Medicare and/or Medicare supplemental plans. If they have a low income, they may qualify for Medicaid. However, other than Medicaid, none of these insurance options provide benefits for long-term care. Therefore, your loved one will need a long-term care insurance policy if they don't want to spend down their assets to be eligible for Medicaid.

Private Health Insurance

In the patchwork of methods that Americans use to pay for Alzheimer's disease care, private health insurance is one of the most significant resources for families, especially if your loved one is under the age of 65. Most health insurance policies will cover medical costs associated with Alzheimer's disease, including doctors' visits, exams, lab tests, and medications. However, private health insurance generally does not cover home healthcare or long-term care. In addition, most insurance policies do not cover pre-existing conditions, so you should not switch your loved one's health insurance policy after their diagnosis if possible. The following checklists address some of the things you should consider regarding private health insurance.

Checklist: Basics about private health insurance

☐ If your loved one already has health insurance, they may have individual or family private insurance, a group employee plan or pension, or retiree coverage. Group plans always have less expensive premiums and often have better benefits than individual policies, although group plans are typically provided by employers and may not be available if your loved one has to quit their job.

☐ If your loved one does not have health insurance, most private health insurance companies offer plans to individuals, although they may be prohibitively expensive. If your loved one has a low income, purchasing a health insurance plan through the Affordable Care Act Marketplace may offer cheaper premiums.

☐ Private health insurance policies differ in monthly premium based on the deductible, co-payments or co-insurance, and type of coverage.

☐ The premium is the monthly amount the policy holder pays to the insurance company in exchange for insurance coverage.

☐ Premiums often depend on the types of services or conditions covered. For example, coverage for pregnancy and childbirth typically increases the premium. If your loved one has pregnancy and childbirth coverage and they are too old to have children, you may ask the insurance company to remove that coverage in exchange for a lower premium.

☐ A deductible is the amount of money the policy holder must pay out-of-pocket for medical expenses before the insurance company will begin to pay. Depending on the plan, deductibles can range from around $500 to over $6,000.

☐ A co-payment (or co-pay) is the amount charged directly to the policy holder for specific medical expenses (e.g., a $20 co-pay for every doctor's appointment).

- [ ] Co-insurance is similar to co-pays, except it is generally a percentage of the total cost (e.g., pay 10% of the cost of prescription medication).

- [ ] Co-payments and co-insurance are usually charged and paid up front at the time the expense is incurred.

- [ ] Many health insurance policies include some type of prescription coverage, although the amount paid out-of-pocket for generic vs. brand name drugs varies widely among insurance policies, medications, insurance companies, and pharmacies.

- [ ] Some private health insurance policies allow the use of a health savings account, through which medical costs can be paid tax free. However, these are usually high-deductible insurance policies with deductibles of $5,000 or more, and the options for this type of policy are limited.

- [ ] Other than the co-pay or co-insurance, most medical facilities and pharmacies will submit your loved one's medical claims to the insurance company on your behalf. The amount that is not covered by the insurance company is then billed to your loved one. Full costs of medical services do not need to be paid at the time of service.

- [ ] Before the Affordable Care Act, most health insurance policies had an annual and/or lifetime maximum. Any medical costs over that maximum were the responsibility of the policy holder. However, now these maximums are not allowed for most new policies. If your loved one has had the same insurance policy for many years, you may want to check if it has any maximum payouts associated with it. If it does have an annual or lifetime maximum, you may want to negotiate with the insurance company to have those limits removed.

If your loved one has trouble paying for medical expenses even with a good health insurance policy in place, talk to the medical facility and work out an affordable payment plan to pay for medical expenses. Most hospitals and clinics are willing to work with you if it means they will eventually get paid.

If your loved one received health insurance through their job and had to quit because of their diagnosis of Alzheimer's disease, they may be able to extend their health insurance coverage through COBRA (Consolidated Omnibus Budget Reconciliation Act) for a limited time. For-profit companies with 20 or more employees and state and local governments that offer a group plan to employees are required to offer COBRA insurance when an employee's insurance coverage would typically end.

Checklist: Basics about COBRA health insurance

☐ COBRA insurance is very expensive. Your loved one will likely have to pay more than they did as an active employee because they will be paying both the employer and employee portions of the premium. In addition, the insurance company may charge an extra 2% for administrative fees and an extra 50% if the individual has a qualifying disability.

☐ COBRA coverage typically extends to all individuals who were previously covered on the insurance plan, including the former employee and the employee's spouse and dependents.

☐ Individuals who are eligible for COBRA insurance have 60 days from the time the employer plan ends to enroll in COBRA.

☐ COBRA coverage typically lasts 18 months, can be extended to 29 months in the event of disability, and can extend to an absolute maximum of 36 months.

☐ If your loved one is eligible for COBRA insurance, you should consider all other health insurance options before you opt for COBRA coverage simply because of the increased cost of premiums. In particular, if your loved one's spouse and/or dependents are listed on the original policy, they should purchase a different policy as soon as possible, especially if they do not have pre-existing conditions.

☐ COBRA insurance is often useful if you plan to purchase a different policy but coverage on the new policy doesn't begin until one or more months after enrollment. In this situation, COBRA coverage would allow the individual or family to have uninterrupted health insurance coverage between plans.

☐ If your loved one decides to waive their right to enroll in COBRA coverage, they are allowed to revoke their waiver any time within the normal period that they would have been allowed continuation coverage (typically 18 months). Continued coverage then begins on the day the waiver is revoked and extends until the end of the original continuation period.

☐ If you terminate COBRA coverage before you have another insurance plan in place, you may not be eligible to receive insurance until the next open enrollment session, which is typically between November and January for most group plans.

☐ If your loved one's family does not want to use COBRA coverage, individuals on the terminated insurance plan have a 30- to 60-day special enrollment eligibility for other plans, starting from the day the insurance policy was terminated. (For example, if a husband was listed on his wife's group plan and the wife was diagnosed with Alzheimer's disease, they would have 30 days to enroll in the husband's group plan, if available.)

Long-Term Care Insurance

Just as a health insurance policy is vital to paying for medical costs associated with Alzheimer's disease, long-term care insurance is vital to paying for living costs associated with Alzheimer's disease, including at-home medical care, assisted living, and memory care unit costs. For a thorough discussion about this topic, see *Long-Term Care Insurance, Power of Attorney, Wealth Management, and Other First Steps*. A few basic concepts related to the cost of long-term care insurance are included in the checklist below.

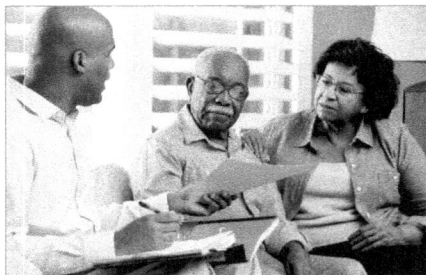

Checklist: Basics about the cost of long-term care insurance

☐ Premiums for long-term care insurance depend on a person's health and age, the policy's waiting period and benefit period, and the amount of the daily benefit, among other factors. Married couples may receive a discount.

☐ The waiting period is the amount of time that must pass between when the individual is eligible for benefits and when the insurance begins paying. This is typically 0, 30, 60, or 90 days. In addition, many insurance companies require that the waiting period include only days that care is received. For example, if your loved one receives at-home care five days per week and has a 30-day waiting period, benefits will begin after six weeks.

- Eligibility for benefits usually depends on your loved one's inability to perform a certain number of activities of daily living (ADL), such as bathing, dressing, eating, or toileting. Most policies state that your loved one must be unable to perform two ADL before eligibility occurs. This is called a benefit trigger.

- The benefit period is the minimum amount of time that the policy will cover your loved one's expenses. This is typically 1, 2, 3, or 5 years.

- The daily benefit is the maximum cost that the policy will cover per day, usually between $50 and $350. Costs above this per day must be paid by the policy holder. The daily benefit is often applied in full for nursing home care, but the insurance company may pay only a portion (usually 50% to 75%) of the daily benefit for other services, such as assisted living or at-home care.

- As an example, say that your loved one has a long-term care insurance policy with a five-year benefit period and a daily benefit of $150 per day. This policy will cover a total of $273,750 (365 days × 5 years × $150/day) in long-term care expenses over five or more years, depending on how long it takes to accrue that level of expenses.

- Once your loved one reaches the maximum benefit under their chosen plan, they will no longer be eligible for payment of long-term care costs under their insurance policy. Therefore, it is vital that your loved one select adequate benefits when they purchase their policy. Keep in mind that memory care units are likely to cost $200–$350/day, so if you or your loved one are concerned about developing Alzheimer's disease, you should select as high a daily benefit as you can afford.

- Annual premiums can range from $1,800 per year to over $5,000 per year for policies with a three-year benefit period and a daily benefit of $150. Premium costs may fall above or below this for policies with different benefit packages.

- If your loved one has already been diagnosed with Alzheimer's disease before they purchase long-term care insurance, they may be denied coverage if a medical examination is required. The premiums may also be cost prohibitive.

Another option for long-term care insurance is to purchase a policy through the state's Partnership program. These programs offer asset protection as well as payment of long-term care costs. However, not all states have a participating Partnership program. Some basics related to the costs of Partnership programs are included in the following checklist. Additional discussion is included in *Long-Term Care Insurance, Power of Attorney, Wealth Management, and Other First Steps*.

Checklist: Basics about state-sponsored Partnership programs

☐ Although they have the additional benefit of asset protection, most state-sponsored long-term care Partnership plans have similar premiums as an equivalent private long-term care insurance policy. However, this may not be true in all states.

☐ Asset protection means that a certain amount of the policy holder's personal assets will be protected from the Medicaid asset requirement. To learn more about Medicaid asset requirements, see Checklist: Medicaid and long-term nursing care coverage.

☐ If your loved one has a Partnership plan with asset protection, they can increase the amount of countable assets they are allowed to have for Medicaid eligibility. This asset protection is associated with the individual's coverage under the Partnership plan.

☐ For example, if your loved one has a three-year benefit period with a $200 daily benefit, they will have benefits and asset protection equaling $219,000 (365 days × 3 years × $200/day). Therefore, if their basic Medicaid asset requirement is less than $2,000, they will be eligible for Medicaid if they have less than $221,000 ($219,000 + $2,000) in total countable assets when the benefits of the Partnership plan are exhausted.

☐ Even with asset protection, individuals with monthly income above Medicaid limits will be required to use their excess income to pay for care in order to qualify for Medicaid. This is called spending down your income.

☐ For wealthy individuals, some states offer a "total" asset protection plan. With a Partnership plan that contains total asset protection, all of your loved one's assets will be protected if they exhaust their long-term care insurance benefits and need to apply for Medicaid. These plans are usually much more expensive than other Partnership plans.

☐ Most states that participate in Partnership programs have reciprocity. This means that if your loved one purchases their Partnership policy in one state and later moves to another state, their new state will honor their Partnership policy, including asset protection. Currently, California is the only state that participates in the Partnership program that does not have reciprocity. However, nine additional states that do not sell Partnership long-term policies also will not honor Partnership policies from other states.

Medicare

For numerous people with Alzheimer's disease, many medical expenses are covered by insurance provided through Medicare. Medicare is a multi-part government insurance program for individuals who are 65 years of age or older, are under the age of 65 with certain disabilities (including Alzheimer's disease if your loved one is no longer able to work), or have end-stage renal disease. Because Alzheimer's disease primarily affects individuals over the age of 65, your loved one is likely qualified for Medicare or is already enrolled in Medicare.

The costs associated with Medicare coverage depend on several factors, including when your loved one enrolled, the type of plan (or plans) chosen, work history, amount of income, medications needed, and providers used. The following checklists provide basic information about Medicare, including information about costs to expect. All costs are based on 2015 estimates. Estimates change each year, so check the Medicare website for the most up-to-date information.

Checklist: Types of Medicare coverage

☐ **Medicare Part A (Hospital Insurance).** Part A covers inpatient hospital stays, care in skilled nursing facilities, hospice care, and some home healthcare.

☐ **Medicare Part B (Medical Insurance).** Part B covers certain doctors' services, outpatient care, medical supplies, and preventive services. (Note: The term "Original Medicare" refers to Part A and/or Part B. These two parts are typically purchased together.)

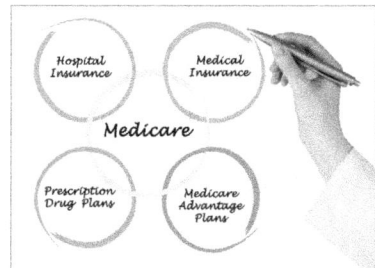

☐ **Medicare Part C (Medicare Advantage Plans).** An Advantage Plan is a type of Medicare plan offered by a private company that contracts with Medicare to provide all of an individual's Part A and Part B benefits. Part C plans may also provide Part D benefits.

☐ **Medicare Part D (Prescription Drug Coverage).** Part D adds prescription drug coverage to Medicare Part A and Part B. Part D plans are offered by private insurance companies approved by Medicare.

Checklist: Basics about Medicare Part A and Part B

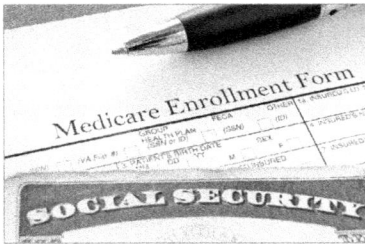

☐ You can find out if your loved one is eligible for Medicare by age by using the government's online calculator. You can also get a premium estimate and find out when the next enrollment period is if your loved one is not already enrolled.

☐ When your loved one enrolls in Medicare, they are automatically signed up for Medicare Part A.

☐ Medicare Part B coverage is optional based on the presence of additional coverage. For example, if your loved one is still working and is receiving health insurance through an employer or a spouse's employer, your loved one can elect to not enroll in Medicare Part B. If your loved one was automatically enrolled in Part B and they want to drop their coverage, they need to follow the instructions on their Medicare card. However, they may have to pay a late enrollment fee if they want to sign up again later.

☐ If your loved one is receiving Social Security checks, they are automatically enrolled in Medicare Part A and Part B. People who qualify for Social Security disability are automatically enrolled two years after their disability is recognized. Individuals who are automatically enrolled will be sent a Medicare card upon enrollment.

☐ If your loved one is not automatically enrolled, they will need to sign up in their Initial Enrollment Period. The seven-month Initial Enrollment Period is open three months before an individual's 65th birthday month, during the birthday month itself, and three months after. For example, an individual with a birthday in August will be eligible for enrollment from May 1 to November 30 in the year of their 65th birthday.

- ☐ If your loved one misses their Initial Enrollment Period, they can sign up during the General Enrollment Period between January 1 and March 31 each year. Your loved one may have to pay a fee for late enrollment.

- ☐ Exceptions to the Initial Enrollment Period and General Enrollment Period occur if your loved one did not enroll in Part B because they were in an employer or union group health plan. In that case, your loved one can sign up for Medicare up to eight months after their coverage with the group health plan ends or after employment ends, whichever happens first. This usually does not incur a late enrollment penalty.

- ☐ Your loved one can apply for Medicare by visiting the Social Security website, going to the local Social Security office, or calling Social Security at 1-800-772-1213.

- ☐ Your loved one cannot be denied Medicare coverage because of their Alzheimer's disease diagnosis. If they are denied coverage and you believe they qualify because of age or disability, they are entitled to an individual analysis of eligibility. Your loved one may have better success obtaining coverage after denial if you ask your loved one's doctor to help.

- ☐ Fill out an Initial Enrollment Questionnaire (IEQ) so that your loved one's healthcare bills are paid correctly and on time. The form asks about other health insurance that might pay before Medicare does, such as group health plan coverage from an employer. Medicare will mail instructions for how to access and fill out this form online. You will need to log in to complete the questionnaire.

- ☐ You can get personalized health insurance counseling at no cost from your local State Health Insurance Assistance Program (SHIP).

- ☐ Once your loved one is enrolled in Medicare, they can no longer contribute to a health savings account (HSA). However, they can still use money from an established HSA to pay for medical expenses until the account is depleted.

Checklist: Costs of Medicare Part A

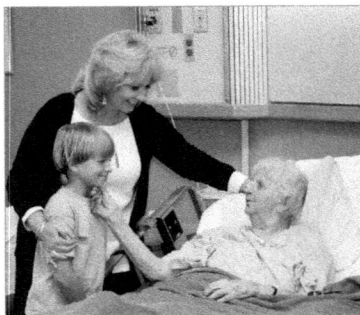

□ If your loved one or their spouse worked at least 10 years in a Medicare-taxable job, your loved one will not be charged a premium for Part A coverage.

□ If your loved one paid Medicare taxes for 30–39 quarters (7.5–9.75 years), their Part A premium will be $224.

□ If your loved one paid Medicare taxes for fewer than 30 quarters, their Part A premium will be $407.

□ Part A premiums may increase by 10% if your loved one didn't enroll during their Initial Enrollment Period. This increase lasts for twice as long as the number of years that they could have been enrolled but weren't.

□ Part A pays for a portion of the services and supplies that Medicare deems medically necessary. If a procedure or treatment is not medically necessary or approved by Medicare, it will not be covered. In addition, if the healthcare facility charges more than Medicare deems reasonable (the "Medicare-approved amount"), your loved one may be required to pay the amount above the Medicare-approved amount.

□ If your loved one requires inpatient care in an acute care hospital, long-term care hospital, or mental hospital, they will have to pay a $1,260 deductible for each benefit period, $0 co-insurance for each benefit period for days 1–60, $315 co-insurance per day of each benefit period for days 61–90, and $630 co-insurance per each "lifetime reserve day" after day 90 for each benefit period. (Each individual has up to 60 lifetime reserve days they can use over their lifetime.) If your loved one requires inpatient hospital care beyond the lifetime reserve days, they will have to pay all costs.

□ For inpatient hospital care, Medicare will generally not cover private-duty nursing, a private room, television and phone in the room, and personal care items. If your loved one wants a private room, they will be responsible for paying the costs associated with that room. However, if a private room is the only room available or offered, then Medicare will pay costs associated with that room.

☐ If your loved one requires skilled nursing care in a skilled nursing facility (SNF) for a limited time, your loved one will pay $0 for the first 20 days, $157.50 for days 21–100, and all costs for days 101 and beyond. However, in order to qualify for these benefits, your loved one must first have a qualified hospital stay of three inpatient days. Outpatient days, such as days spent in the ER for observation, do not count toward the three days.

☐ If your loved one is released from the SNF and re-enters the SNF in 30 days or fewer, they do not need another qualifying hospital stay for Medicare to pay SNF costs. Coverage days begin where the previous stay left off. For example, if your loved one was in the SNF for 15 days on their last stay, their new stay will start on day 16 of coverage.

☐ If your loved one is released from the SNF and re-enters the SNF in 31 to 59 days, they need a new three-day hospital stay to qualify for Medicare coverage. However, coverage days still begin where the previous stay left off.

☐ If your loved one is released from the SNF and re-enters the SNF after 60 days, they will need a new three-day hospital stay to qualify for coverage, but the SNF coverage starts over at day one.

☐ If your loved one needs intermittent at-home skilled nursing care or therapy (physical, occupational, speech), Medicare will pay 100% of physician-ordered home healthcare services and 80% of the Medicare-approved amount for medical equipment. However, this does not include 24-hour-a-day at-home care, meals, homemaker services, or personal care; and the individual's condition must be expected to improve over a reasonable period of time. Therefore, individuals with Alzheimer's disease may not be eligible for these benefits.

☐ Medicare Part A covers nursing home costs only if your loved one requires skilled nursing care (e.g., changing sterile bandages). Medicare does not generally pay for nursing home care if your loved one only needs custodial care (e.g., help with walking, bathing, etc.).

☐ If your loved one's doctor certifies that your loved one has six months or less to live, your loved one will be eligible for hospice care coverage under Medicare. Your loved one pays $0 for hospice care, but they may need to pay a co-payment of $5 or less for prescription medications that relieve symptoms. Once your loved one is on hospice care, Medicare no longer pays for treatment intended to cure a terminal illness, room and board at long-term care facilities, or care in an emergency room or hospital.

Checklist: Costs of Medicare Part B

☐ The premium for Part B depends on marital status, tax filing status if married, and income range.

☐ For single individuals with an annual income of $85,000 or less, the Part B premium is $104.90 per month. The premium increases as income increases. The highest rate for single individuals with an annual income of $214,000 or more is $335.70.

☐ Married couples who file taxes jointly have similar premiums as single individuals, but the income amount is doubled. For example, if the couple makes $170,000 or less, their premium will be $104.90, and if they make $428,000 or more, their premium will be $335.70.

☐ Married couples who file taxes separately reach the maximum premium ($335.70) with an individual income of only $129,000.

☐ If your loved one did not sign up during the Initial Enrollment Period or during a Special Enrollment Period, they may be assessed a late enrollment penalty. The monthly premium may increase by as much as 10% for every 12-month period that they could have had Part B but didn't.

☐ Similar to Part A, Part B coverage only extends to services and supplies that are deemed medically necessary. This includes some preventive services. Examples of covered services include doctor visits, lab tests, surgeries, ambulance services, durable medical equipment, and mental health care.

☐ Your loved one will likely pay nothing for most preventive services if they have Part B. Examples of preventive services include an annual wellness visit;

vaccines for the flu, pneumonia and hepatitis B; screenings for cancer, diabetes, depression, sexually transmitted infections, cardiovascular disease, and others; glaucoma tests; nutrition services; and others.

☐ For most other medical services, your loved one will be responsible for paying 20% of the Medicare-approved amount after they have met their deductible. The Part B deductible is $147 per year.

☐ Some services, such as speech, occupational, and physical therapy, have a maximum payout amount. This maximum payout is $1,940 for speech and physical therapy combined and $1,940 for occupational therapy. Some individuals may qualify for an exception to this maximum.

☐ In order for Medicare to cover durable medical equipment, the equipment must be prescribed by a Medicare-approved physician and provided by a Medicare-approved supplier. In addition, Medicare may dictate whether you rent or buy the equipment. Examples of covered medical equipment include blood sugar monitors and test strips, mobility aids (e.g., crutches, canes, wheelchairs, walkers), hospital beds, infusion pumps and supplies, and oxygen equipment.

☐ For mental health services provided by a hospital outpatient clinic or department, your loved one may have to pay an additional co-payment or co-insurance amount to the hospital, which is usually between 20% and 40% of the Medicare-approved amount.

☐ Your loved one may be partially covered for medical expenses associated with a clinical study if they decide to participate in one. If your loved one participates in a clinical trial, discuss costs with both the study facilitators and Medicare to determine which costs will be covered.

Checklist: Basics about Medicare Part C

☐ Medicare Part C plans are offered by private insurance companies rather than the government.

☐ Before enrolling in Part C, your loved one must first enroll in Part A and Part B to confirm eligibility. Then they may choose a Part C plan.

☐ At a minimum, the law requires Part C plans to cover the same services covered by Part A and Part B.

☐ In addition to hospital and medical costs, Part C may cover extra services that are not covered under Part A and Part B, such as dental, vision, and hearing.

☐ Most Part C plans also offer prescription drug coverage.

☐ Similar to private insurance plans, Medicare Part C plans usually allow your loved one to choose one primary care provider; their access to other providers and specialists is restricted based on which physicians are in the plan's network. If your loved one uses a provider outside the network, they will usually pay more than for services provided by an in-network provider.

☐ If your loved one wants to regularly use an out-of-network provider, consider choosing a private fee-for-service plan, which allows you to pay a set fee for each service. However, this may still be more expensive and will likely require extra paperwork for you.

Checklist: Costs of Medicare Part C

☐ Unlike Part A and Part B, Medicare Part C prices vary based on the provider and plan benefits, similar to private insurance plans. However, the cost generally includes the Part B premium as described above plus a Part C additional premium. The Part C premium may range from $0 to over $150.

☐ Factors that affect the premium for Medicare Part C include the amount of the deductible, the types of services your loved one signs up for, and the co-payments associated with the plan.

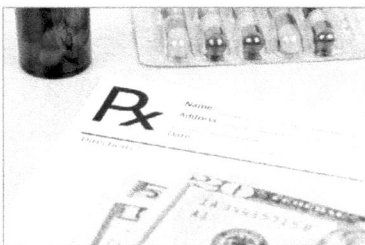

☐ Factors affecting out-of-pocket costs include the amount of co-payments and deductible, whether the plan pays Part B premiums, whether your loved one uses in-network providers, the plan's yearly maximal out-of-pocket costs, and others.

Checklist: Basics about Medicare Part D

☐ Medicare offers optional prescription drug coverage to everyone enrolled in Medicare. If your loved one decides not to sign up for Medicare Part D when they are first eligible and they don't have other creditable prescription drug coverage, they will likely pay a late enrollment penalty if they opt to enroll later.

☐ Similar to Part C, Part D plans are provided by private insurance companies. These plans add drug coverage for individuals with Medicare Part A and Part B. Different plans vary in premium cost and in the drugs they cover.

☐ Each Part D plan has its own list of covered drugs (called a formulary). Many Medicare drug plans place medications into different "tiers" on their formularies. Drugs in each tier have a different cost.

☐ If your loved one has a Medicare Advantage Plan (Part C), they cannot get prescription drug coverage through Part D. Instead, they can add prescription drug coverage directly through their Part C plan. If they want to enroll in Part D, they will be disenrolled from their Part C plan and returned to a regular Part A/Part B plan.

☐ Once your loved one chooses a Medicare drug plan, they can apply by enrolling in the Medicare Plan Finder, visiting the plan's website, completing a paper enrollment form, calling the plan, or calling 1-800-MEDICARE (1-800-633-4227).

Checklist: Costs of Medicare Part D

☐ Costs for Medicare Part D depend on which private insurance company carries the plan and which plan you choose within that company.

☐ Part D plans usually have a monthly premium. Monthly premiums may be increased if your loved one's gross income is above a certain limit based on tax returns two years ago. Therefore, the adjusted premium may change each year depending on your loved one's income. Individuals with an income of $85,000 or less will not have to pay this extra premium. The maximum extra premium is $70.80 per month for individuals with an income above $214,000. This adjusted amount is paid to Medicare, not to the drug plan.

- [ ] Your loved one will be responsible for paying a co-pay or co-insurance for each prescription. This amount will depend on which tier the specific medication is in. Generic drugs are generally in a lower tier than brand-name drugs and thus have a lower co-pay or co-insurance amount.

- [ ] Medicare Part D only covers select drugs, so your loved one may also be responsible for costs of medications that are not included in Medicare Part D.

- [ ] Some plans also have a deductible that your loved one will need to pay before the plan begins covering drug costs. The maximum deductible allowed is $320 in 2015 ($360 in 2016).

- [ ] Part D covers up to a specified amount for prescription medications. When your loved one reaches this limit, they will enter the "donut hole" or coverage gap, in which they will have to pay a higher amount for prescription drugs until they reach their out-of-pocket maximum.

- [ ] Initially, Medicare Part D will cover up to $2,960 (the 2015 limit; $3,310 in 2016) in prescription medication costs. This includes both out-of-pocket costs and the portion of prescriptions that Part D pays. During this time, your loved one will still be responsible for paying their deductible and any co-insurance or co-payments.

- [ ] Once your loved one and their plan have paid $2,960 in prescription costs, your loved one will enter the donut hole. In the donut hole, payment rules differ for covered brand-name drugs and generic drugs.

- [ ] While in the donut hole, your loved one must pay 45% of what Medicare would have reimbursed the pharmacy for a covered brand-name drug. For example, if your loved one needs a brand-name prescription that would normally cost Medicare $75 per month, your loved one will have to pay $33.75 per month for that prescription while in the donut hole. Although your loved one only pays 45% of the brand-name drug cost, 95% of the drug cost will be applied to your loved one's out-of-pocket maximum to help them get out of the donut hole.

- [ ] The policy is different for generic drugs. For generic medications, your loved one must pay 65% of the drug cost while in the donut hole. Medicare will pay the remaining 35%. The entire cost that your loved one pays for generic drugs (65%) will be applied toward their total out-of-pocket maximum to help them get out of the coverage gap.

☐ The amount your loved one has to pay for generic drugs when in the donut hole will decrease each year until it reaches 25% in 2020.

☐ Once your loved one has paid $4,700 (2015 limit) in out-of-pocket prescription costs in one year, including deductibles, co-insurance, and co-payments, they will enter catastrophic coverage. In catastrophic coverage, your loved one will be responsible for only a small co-insurance or co-payment for prescription medications.

☐ If your loved one has reached the coverage gap and is not receiving discounts on their prescriptions, review their policy or contact their insurance company about their prescription drug plan. If the plan doesn't agree that a discount is owed, your loved one can file an appeal.

If your loved one has trouble paying for their medical costs associated with Medicare, several resources are available to help cover costs such as premiums, deductibles, co-insurance, co-payments, and long-term care. These programs include Medigap insurance, Extra Help, and Medicare Savings Programs. The checklists in the following section provide basic information about each of these programs.

Checklist: Basics about Medicare supplemental insurance (Medigap insurance)

☐ Medigap can help pay some healthcare costs that Medicare Part A and Part B don't cover. To be covered, a person must also have Part A and Part B. Medigap insurance is not available to individuals with Medicare Part C.

☐ Similar to Medicare Part C and Part D, Medicare supplemental (Medigap) insurance is sold by private insurance companies. Medigap is not a government program.

☐ A Medigap policy is different from a Medicare Advantage Plan (Part C). Whereas Advantage Plans are an alternative way to get Medicare benefits, Medigap policies only add coverage to a person's Plan A and Plan B benefits.

- ☐ A Medigap policy only covers one person. Each individual must select and pay for their own Medigap plan.

- ☐ Each individual is only allowed to select one Medigap plan. Insurance companies are not allowed to sell more than one Medigap plan to an individual.

- ☐ Insurance companies are not allowed to sell a Medigap policy to individuals who participate in the Medicare Savings Program or have coverage through Medicaid.

- ☐ Individuals who have Medicare coverage based on a disability who are under the age of 65 may not be eligible for Medigap insurance.

- ☐ When purchasing a Medigap policy, first decide which benefits your loved one needs, then decide which of Medigap plans A–N best meets those needs. These plans are standardized (except in Massachusetts, Minnesota, and Wisconsin), so each letter plan should offer the same benefits in different states and through different insurance companies.

- ☐ Each Medigap plan offers a different set of benefits, filling different gaps in Medicare Part A and Part B. Depending on the gaps that most affect your loved one, one Medigap plan may be more beneficial than another plan.

- ☐ Depending on the Medigap plan selected, the plan may cover all or part of your loved one's Part A and Part B deductible, Part A and Part B co-insurance and co-payments, costs above the Medicare-approved amount, and inpatient hospital costs above the Medicare maximum.

- ☐ Medigap policies generally don't cover long-term care, vision or dental care, hearing aids, eyeglasses, private-duty nursing, or prescription drug costs.

- ☐ When choosing a Medigap plan, take time to think about what type of coverage your loved one might need in the future. Unless your coverage ends for a variety of reasons (such as the insurance company going out of business, the plan no longer being offered, or moving out of the coverage area for the plan), the options for switching Medigap plans are limited. Therefore, your loved one needs to select the policy that will best fit their needs long term.

☐ Once you have selected the Medigap plan that is right for your loved one, you can view companies that offer that plan and get contact information for each company.

☐ Most insurance companies only sell some of the Medigap plans, so make sure the company you contact sells the plan your loved one needs. Carefully read any information you are given about the policy and its benefits and costs, and don't be afraid to ask questions if you don't understand something.

☐ Medigap premiums must be paid in addition to Part A and Part B premiums. Different states and different insurance companies offer different premium rates for the same plan with the same benefits, so it is important to shop around before purchasing a policy.

☐ Make sure you understand the insurance company's pricing system for premiums. Some companies use community-rated pricing, in which everyone pays the same amount regardless of age; premium increases are based on inflation, not on age. Some companies use issue-age-rated pricing, in which the premium cost depends on your age when you initially purchase the plan; additional premium increases are based on inflation, not on age. Some companies use attained-age-rated pricing, in which the premium increases each year based on age.

☐ Each individual has a one-time grace period for enrolling in a Medigap plan. This grace period starts on the first day of the month in which the individual is both 65 years old or older AND is enrolled in Medicare Part B. This open enrollment period extends for a total of six months.

☐ During the open enrollment period, insurance companies cannot deny coverage to your loved one for a pre-existing condition. If your loved one does not enroll in a Medigap plan during this grace period, insurance companies have the right to deny them coverage or to charge more for the policy based on the applicant's health status.

☐ Although insurance companies cannot deny coverage to an individual during the open enrollment period due to pre-existing health conditions, they can delay coverage of those pre-existing conditions. This waiting period is generally six months before they will begin to cover medical expenses related to the pre-existing condition. However, Medicare Part A and Part B will still cover expenses related to pre-existing conditions during this waiting period.

☐ Once your loved one has a Medigap policy, the insurance company cannot cancel the policy based on health conditions as long as your loved one continues to pay the premiums.

☐ For more information about Medigap, see http://www.medicare.gov/pubs/pdf/02110.pdf.

When applying for my dad's Medigap insurance, I was overwhelmed by the number of choices that needed to be made. I called AARP to ask for assistance, and they were very helpful. SHIP (State Health Insurance Assistance Program) also provides assistance in choosing a Medigap plan. If you don't understand your options, resources are available to help answer your questions and walk you through your choices.

Checklist: Basics about Extra Help

☐ Just as Medigap helps cover the gap for Medicare Part A and Part B, Extra Help helps cover the gap for Medicare Part D for eligible individuals.

☐ Extra Help assists individuals in paying for Medicare Part D premiums, deductibles, and co-insurance or co-payments.

☐ If your loved one is on an Extra Help plan, they will never enter the Plan D "donut hole."

☐ Your loved one must provide documentation of financial hardship to qualify for Extra Help (assets of $13,640 or less and yearly income of $17,655 or less for a single individual or combined assets of $27,250 or less and yearly income of $23,895 or less for a couple).

☐ When determining eligibility, cash accounts, stocks, and bonds count as assets. A primary home, one vehicle, personal belongings, and some money set aside for burial expenses are not counted as assets.

☐ Because eligibility depends on assets and income, your loved one's eligibility status may change each year if their assets and/or income change.

- [ ] If your loved one is covered by Medicaid or Supplemental Security Income (SSI), they are automatically eligible for Extra Help.

- [ ] If your loved one is not eligible for Extra Help, they can still purchase a Medicare Part D prescription drug plan.

- [ ] In most states, individuals enrolled in Extra Help will pay no more than $2.65 for each generic medication and $6.60 for each brand-name medication that is covered by Medicare. These cheaper medication costs save individuals an average of $4,000 per year, but they will still have to pay regular price for medications not covered by Medicare.

- [ ] Your loved one can apply for Extra Help by going to the Social Security website or calling Social Security at 1-800-772-1213.

Checklist: Basics about Medicare Savings Programs

- [ ] Medicare Savings Programs help individuals with low income and assets pay their Part A premium, Part B premium, and/or Part A and Part B deductibles, co-insurance, and co-payments.

- [ ] The four Medicare Savings Programs have different eligibility requirements and benefits: Qualified Medicare Beneficiary (QMB) Program, Specified Low-Income Medicare Beneficiary (SLMB) Program, Qualifying Individual (QI) Program, and Qualified Disabled and Working Individuals (QDWI) Program.

- [ ] The QMB Program helps pay for Part A and Part B premiums, deductibles, co-insurance, and co-payments for individuals with a monthly income of no more than $1,001 and assets of no more than $7,280 and couples with a monthly income of no more than $1,348 and assets of no more than $10,930.

- [ ] The SLMB Program helps pay Part B premiums for individuals with a monthly income of no more than $1,197 and assets of no more than $7,280 and couples with a monthly income of no more than $1,613 and assets of no more than $10,930.

- [ ] The QI Program helps pay Part B premiums for individuals with a monthly income of no more than $1,345 and assets of no more than $7,280 and couples with a monthly income of no more than $1,813 and assets of no more than $10,930. If your loved one qualifies for the QI program, they must apply every year, and applications are granted on a first-come, first-served basis. Priority is given to people who received QI benefits the previous year. Individuals receiving Medicaid benefits cannot receive QI benefits.

☐ The QDWI Program helps pay Part A premiums for individuals with a monthly income of no more than $1,962 and assets of no more than $4,000 and couples with a monthly income of no more than $2,655 and assets of no more than $6,000. This program is for working individuals who are disabled and are under the age of 65, who lost their premium-free Part A when they went back to work, and who aren't getting state medical assistance.

☐ Individuals who qualify for Extra Help should apply for a Medicare Savings Program, and individuals who qualify for a Medicare Savings Program are automatically eligible for Extra Help.

☐ Similar to Extra Help, countable assets include cash accounts, stocks, and bonds. Countable assets do not include a primary residence, one vehicle, personal belongings, and some money set aside for burial expenses. Some states count assets and income differently, so if your loved one needs help paying for their Medicare expenses, apply for a Medicare Savings Program to determine their eligibility.

☐ To apply for a Medicare Savings Program, call your state Medicaid program.

Medicaid

Individuals on Medicare and other supplemental insurance programs as well as individuals under the age of 65 may be eligible for Medicaid if they meet certain income and/or asset requirements. Medicaid is a government-funded health insurance program for low-income individuals and families who meet certain income and asset requirements. Individuals who cannot pay for traditional health insurance can apply for help from Medicaid to pay their medical and hospital bills. Qualified individuals may also receive help with long-term care costs, but the requirements for these benefits are very strict. Determining eligibility and applying for Medicaid may seem complicated, but finding out whether your loved one qualifies for benefits can pay off both immediately and in the long run.

Checklist: Basics about Medicaid

☐ Medicaid is a health insurance program for individuals with low income and few assets.

☐ Medicaid is funded jointly by the federal and state governments and is administered by state governments. Therefore, different states may have different services and requirements for their Medicaid program. However, each state must provide at least minimum benefits as outlined by the federal government.

☐ Similar to Medicare, Medicaid provides hospital and medical insurance for qualified individuals. However, individuals with full Medicaid benefits also receive a wider array of services, including long-term nursing care. Some states may also cover dental, eye, and hearing services.

☐ If your loved one is diagnosed with Alzheimer's disease at a young age, has to quit their job, and still has children under the age of 21 at home, the children may be eligible for health insurance through CHIP (Children's Health Insurance Program) depending on family income requirements, even if the adults in the family are not eligible. CHIP is essentially the children's division of Medicaid.

☐ You can enroll in Medicaid at any point during the year. To determine if your loved one may be eligible for Medicaid, use Medicaid's online screener.

☐ If your loved one qualifies for Medicaid, you have two options for applying. The first is to apply directly to your loved one's state agency after determining their eligibility online. With this option, coverage can begin immediately. The other option is to fill out a Marketplace application online. These applications are open only from mid-November through mid-February.

Checklist: Medicaid regulations for individuals under 65

☐ For individuals under the age of 65, the sole determining factor for basic Medicaid eligibility is the individual or family's modified adjusted gross income, or MAGI. To qualify for Medicaid, the individual or family's MAGI must be under a certain percentage of the federal poverty level (FPL), usually 133% of the FPL or less. In 2015, the FPL for one individual is a monthly income of $980.83, whereas the FPL for a family of four is a monthly income of $2,020.83.

☐ Because some states provide Medicaid coverage for individuals with incomes above 133% of the poverty level, they can choose to require monthly premiums, co-payments, co-insurance, and deductibles for these higher-income individuals. However, these costs are usually minimal compared to private insurance plans.

☐ Individuals who are under age 65 and don't meet Medicaid income requirements may still be eligible for Medicaid if they are deemed "medically needy."

☐ Medically needy individuals can qualify for Medicaid on a month-to-month basis depending on their medical bills. If these bills are high enough to reduce the individual's usable income below the income amount allowed by their state, they are eligible to qualify for Medicaid through the Excess Income Program.

☐ In the Excess Income Program, individuals can submit medical bills to Medicaid to become eligible for Medicaid. The amount of medical bills that must be submitted depends on the individual's income level. For example, an individual who has a monthly income that is $50 above their MAGI limit will have to prove that they have $50 or more in medical bills for that month. Once they prove they have hit that limit, they are eligible for Medicaid benefits for their remaining medical expenses for that month. Some states may also require an asset limit before a medically needy individual is eligible for Medicaid.

☐ Paid medical bills can be applied to the excess income for up to six months. For example, if your loved one has excess income of $50 and they paid $25 in medical bills in July and $25 in medical bills in August, they can combine those two months to be eligible for Medicaid for the remainder of August or for any month through December. Similarly, if your loved one paid $200 in medical bills in September with excess income of $50 per month, they will qualify for Medicaid for any four-month time span between September and February.

☐ Unpaid medical bills can be applied to meet the excess income requirement in any month as long as the bills are still viable (i.e., the medical facility still expects payment). If using unpaid medical bills to qualify for Medicaid, Medicaid will not pay the qualifying bills. They will cover any bills in addition to those qualifying bills, similar to a deductible.

☐ When using medical bills to spend down excess income to qualify for Medicaid, medical bills can only be used once. Your loved one cannot use both an unpaid bill and proof of payment for that same bill to qualify for Medicaid in two different months.

☐ Bills that can be used to spend down excess income include health insurance premiums, deductibles, co-insurance, co-payments, and other medical expenses.

☐ If your loved one wants to have consistent Medicaid coverage, they can pay Medicaid their excess income each month, similar to an insurance premium. They will then be eligible for Medicaid benefits.

☐ Some states require that medically needy individuals fulfill their excess income spend-down for multiple months before they will cover inpatient hospital care. For example, if your loved one has $50 in excess monthly income, they would have to accumulate $300 in inpatient hospital bills before Medicaid coverage of in-patient hospital costs would begin. Your loved one would then be eligible for Medicaid coverage for six months.

Checklist: Medicaid regulations for individuals over 65 (dual-eligible)

☐ Dual-eligible individuals qualify for both Medicare and Medicaid. Generally, these are individuals over age 65 with low income and few assets. However, individuals who qualify for Medicare based on a disability or end-stage renal disease may be under the age of 65.

☐ For dual-eligible individuals, the MAGI rule for Medicaid eligibility does not apply. Dual-eligible individuals must meet both income and asset requirements to qualify for Medicaid.

☐ To qualify for full Medicaid benefits, including long-term care coverage, individuals must meet asset and income requirements as determined by the state. For more on these requirements, see Checklist: Medicaid and long-term nursing care coverage.

☐ Individuals who do not meet the requirements for full Medicaid benefits may be eligible for Medicaid support through a Medicare Savings Program with its established income and asset requirements. These individuals may receive help paying for their Part A, Part B, and Part D premiums, deductibles, co-insurance, and co-payments but not long-term care costs.

☐ In addition to services covered through Medicare, individuals who qualify for Medicaid may have access to additional benefits above the normal Medicare benefits, including prescription drug coverage and coverage for eyeglasses and hearing aids.

Checklist: Medicaid and long-term nursing care coverage

☐ For all individuals who require nursing home care (both MAGI-eligible and dual-eligible), Medicaid has strict income and asset requirements before they will begin to pay for long-term care.

☐ Generally, income requirements are similar to MAGI rules (133% of FPL or less). Asset requirements are usually $2,000 or less of accumulated assets for an individual or $3,000 or less for a couple. These requirements vary widely among states, so check with your loved one's local Social Security office to determine the requirements for their state.

☐ Assets that count toward the asset limit include cash accounts, investments, some real estate, and some retirement accounts. Assets that generally do not count toward your loved one's asset limits include their primary home, one vehicle, and personal possessions. Other assets and income that count toward the asset limit may vary by state.

☐ In order to qualify for full Medicaid nursing home coverage, some individuals may need to "spend down" their income and assets.

☐ The income spend-down is similar to the spend-down for medically needy individuals. Your loved one will be required to use their excess monthly income to pay for medical and long-term care costs, and once that amount is spent, Medicaid will cover the rest of the costs.

☐ Spend-down of assets is strictly regulated by Medicaid. Individuals are allowed to spend down their assets for normal living and medical expenses without incurring a Medicaid penalty. They are not allowed to spend down assets simply by giving away their assets to others. Assets that are given away will be subject to a five-year "look back" period.

☐ During the look back period, if the Medicaid applicant has given away assets to children, grandchildren, or others, these gifts can be counted against them for Medicaid eligibility. For example, if your loved one gave each of three grandchildren $10,000 two years ago and your loved applies for Medicaid now, they will incur a $30,000 penalty for long-term care coverage if they are otherwise eligible to receive Medicaid.

☐ Your loved one's Medicaid penalty, if they have one, will be assessed based on their monthly expenses. For example, if your loved one has a Medicaid penalty of $30,000 and expects to need $5,000 per month for long-term nursing care, Medicaid will not pay for the first six months ($30,000/$5,000 = 6).

☐ Asset transfers that do not incur a Medicaid penalty include transfers to a spouse up to a certain limit, a child who is blind or has a disability, a trust for the benefit of a child who is blind or has a disability, or a trust for the sole benefit of an individual under age 65 who has a disability.

☐ If your loved one incurs a penalty period, the penalty period will not apply until your loved one moves into a nursing home, has spent down their assets based on Medicaid stipulations, applies for Medicaid, and is approved for coverage. Once all these conditions are met, the penalty period will start; once the penalty period is over, Medicaid will begin paying nursing home costs.

☐ Because medical expenses, especially long-term nursing care expenses, can cost as much as $5,000 to $8,000 per month or more, Medicaid allows some individuals needing this level of care to be eligible for Medicaid at a higher income or asset level if paying for these services out-of-pocket would cause undue hardship for their spouse. This is called spousal impoverishment.

☐ Under Medicaid's spousal impoverishment provisions, a certain amount of a couple's combined resources are protected for use by the spouse still living in the community. Depending on the couple's needs, the monthly maintenance needs allowance for the spouse in the community is between $1,991.25 and $2,980.50, the monthly housing allowance is $597.38, the available assets are between $23,844 and $119,220, and the home equity limits are between $552,000 and $828,000. Any shared income or resources above these limits must be used to pay for long-term care before Medicaid begins to pay for care (i.e., the couple must spend down their excess income and assets).

☐ If your loved one with Alzheimer's disease is in the nursing home and their spouse does not have enough personal income to meet their monthly maintenance needs allowance, your loved one in the nursing home can transfer assets to their spouse up to the allowance amount rather than using that income to pay for nursing home costs.

☐ For individuals with Medicaid coverage who need long-term nursing care, they may have limited choices for which nursing home they can use. Specifically, Medicaid will only cover services provided in a nursing home that is licensed and certified as a Medicaid Nursing Facility. However, if your loved one is already in a nursing home when they become eligible for Medicaid, usually Medicaid and the nursing facility do not require your loved one to move to a new facility if their current facility is not a certified Medicaid Nursing Facility.

☐ If your loved one has Medicaid coverage and they are not yet in a nursing home, they may be placed on a waiting list for a Medicaid Nursing Facility, because the number of "Medicaid beds" might be limited in their preferred nursing home.

Checklist: Medicaid Estate Recovery program

☐ If your loved one receives Medicaid coverage for long-term nursing home care and is over the age of 55, their estate may be subject to the Medicaid Estate Recovery program after their death.

☐ The Medicaid Estate Recovery program allows Medicaid to make claims on your loved one's possessions to recover the cost of your loved one's care for nursing facility services, home and community-based services, and related hospital and prescription drug services. About half of the states recover payments for all Medicaid services, not just long-term care-related services.

☐ Your loved one's remaining debts (mortgage, credit card debt, unpaid utility bills, etc.) receive higher priority for payment than the Medicaid Estate Recovery program. Medicaid can only claim what's left of the estate after these debts have been paid.

☐ Medicaid can only claim up to the amount that they paid out for services. If your loved one's estate has greater value than their Medicaid claims, Medicaid cannot recover the entirety of your loved one's estate.

☐ In some states, possessions that pass to a beneficiary without going through probate court may be exempt from recovery by Medicaid. This includes jointly-held assets, assets in a living trust, or life estates. However, different states have different rules about the definition of "estate" and whether non-probate assets are recoverable, so check with your loved one's state policy to determine which assets may be subject to Medicaid recovery.

☐ Because of the Medicaid asset restrictions, the most substantial asset that your loved one is likely to own at the time of their death is their primary residence.

☐ Medicaid may require that your loved one's home be sold for repayment of Medicaid benefits. However, the home is protected if a spouse, child under the age of 21, child of any age who is blind or has a disability, sibling with equity interest in the home, or adult child who provided at least two years of caregiving services before Medicaid eligibility still lives in the home. Property may also be protected if it is income-generating for heirs, such as a farm, rental property, or family business. However, if the surviving spouse is the only one with a claim to the home, Medicaid may come back after the spouse's death and recover the cost of the home.

☐ Medicaid is also allowed to place a lien on your loved one's home or other real estate so that when the real estate is sold before or after your loved one's death, Medicaid can collect repayment from the proceeds of the sale.

☐ Medicaid may waive their right to recovery if recovery of your loved one's estate may cause undue hardship for the individual's heirs. This undue hardship is defined differently in each state, and heirs often have to request the waiver during the probate process.

☐ Family members of your loved one should not be expected to repay Medicaid with their own money unless they received assets from your loved one's estate. Then, only assets received from the estate are subject to recovery. Other personal possessions, assets, and income are not subject to recovery. However, if Medicaid has placed a lien on the individual's home and the family wants to keep the home in the family, they may have to repay Medicaid for the cost of the house from their personal funds.

As you can see, government health insurance regulations and eligibility requirements are very confusing, and many programs differ depending on state regulations. If you think your loved one may qualify for one of these programs, call your local Social Security office to discuss their eligibility and to sign up for each program.

Another program run through Medicaid that may benefit your loved one is PACE (Program of All-Inclusive Care for the Elderly). This program is designed to help your loved one live in the community as long as possible rather than having to live in an assisted living or long-term care facility. PACE programs are only offered in limited areas, so check with your local Medicaid office to determine whether a PACE program is available in your area.

Checklist: Basics about PACE (Program of All-Inclusive Care for the Elderly)

☐ PACE is a healthcare program that provides comprehensive care to enable individuals to meet their healthcare needs in the community rather than in a long-term care facility.

☐ To be eligible for PACE, your loved one must be 55 years old or older, live in a PACE service area, need nursing home-level care, and be able to live safely in the community with the help of PACE.

☐ Individuals enrolled in PACE receive care and services in the home, the community, and/or the local PACE center. The PACE center has local contracts with physicians and other providers to deliver the care that is needed. Individuals in the PACE program are required to use participating PACE providers.

☐ Each individual is cared for by a small number of people, so the caregivers really get to know the individual and their needs.

☐ PACE covers services including adult day care, dentistry, emergency services, home care, hospital care, preventive care, meals, medical specialty services, nursing home care, nutritional counseling, occupational and physical therapy, prescription drugs, transportation to the PACE center as needed, and respite care for caregivers.

☐ If your loved one is enrolled in PACE, they do not need to enroll in Medicare Part D. All of their prescription drugs will be provided through PACE.

☐ The premium for PACE depends on your loved one's financial situation. If they are enrolled in Medicaid, they won't have to pay a monthly premium. If they are not eligible for Medicaid but they have Medicare, they will be charged a monthly premium to cover long-term care and the Part D benefit. If they do not have Medicare or Medicaid, they can pay for PACE privately.

☐ Once enrolled in PACE, the premium will not increase even if your loved one needs more care and services.

☐ Individuals who are enrolled in PACE do not pay any deductibles or co-payments for any drug, service, or care provided by the PACE healthcare team. Care provided by individuals outside the PACE team will need to be paid by the individual or other insurance policy.

☐ Individuals enrolled in PACE can leave the program at any time.

☐ To apply for PACE, contact your state Medicaid office.

Disability Insurance

If your loved one was still working at the time of their diagnosis, they may have disability insurance either through their employer or through private insurance. Depending on the stage of your loved one's Alzheimer's disease and whether they had to quit their job because of the effects of Alzheimer's disease, disability insurance may provide another source of income for your loved one. Note that the amount your loved one will receive from their disability insurance payouts is often dependent on their salary at the time of disability, so your loved one should not continue to pay premiums for disability insurance if they are no longer working and receiving a salary. The checklist below contains basic information about receiving benefits from disability insurance. For more information about purchasing disability insurance, see *Long-Term Care Insurance, Power of Attorney, Wealth Management, and Other First Steps*.

Checklist: Basics about private disability income insurance

- ☐ Private disability income insurance provides income for a person who must stop working due to injury or illness. However, some disability insurance policies only cover accidental injury and not illness, so make sure you check your loved one's policy to see if they qualify for benefits.

- ☐ Some disability insurance policies provided by an employer only cover disability due to on-the-job injuries. Therefore, your loved one with Alzheimer's disease would not qualify to receive benefits from this type of policy.

- ☐ Disability insurance policies can provide coverage for either short-term disability or long-term disability.

- ☐ For both types of disability insurance, your loved one must meet disability requirements before their elimination period can begin, and then the elimination period must end before they begin receiving benefits.

- ☐ If your loved one has short-term disability insurance, the elimination period is usually between 0 and 90 days. Short-term disability policies usually provide no more than two years of benefits.

- ☐ If your loved one has long-term disability insurance, the elimination period is usually between 90 and 365 days, and they may pay benefits from two years up to the time the individual reaches the age of 67, depending on the policy your loved one selected.

- ☐ Policies paid for by employers generally provide 60% to 80% of the covered person's gross income. These benefits are taxed.

☐ If your loved one bought a personal disability income policy (as opposed to a policy provided by an employer), the benefits will be paid out at the level they chose. These benefits are not taxed.

☐ Most insurance companies will waive the premium once your loved one begins collecting payouts from the policy. If they are still expecting premium payments after benefits begin, call the insurance company to see if they will waive those costs.

Life Insurance

If your loved one has a short-term need for cash to pay for care costs, a life insurance policy can provide a valuable source of income. However, using life insurance for cash comes with many drawbacks, from insurance company penalties and fees to a reduction in the value of the policy. In addition, your loved one can only borrow from permanent or whole life insurance, not term life insurance. This checklist outlines the four major methods of using an insurance policy for cash: making a withdrawal, taking a loan, surrendering the policy, and making a viatical (or life) settlement. Before taking any of these steps, be sure to talk to a qualified insurance advisor.

Checklist: Basics about borrowing from a life insurance policy

☐ **Withdrawal.** Typically, your loved one will be able to withdraw cash they have paid into the policy over time. If taken in small amounts, these withdrawals are not taxable. Drawbacks of withdrawals include reduction in the value of the policy's death or survivor benefit (i.e., the amount survivors will receive), the possibility of increased income taxes, and the possibility of increased insurance premiums to maintain the same death benefit.

☐ **Loan.** If your loved one has permanent, or whole, life insurance, they can borrow some of the money they have paid into it over time. The major drawback of loans is that the value of the death benefit will be reduced if you do not pay back the loan by returning money to the policy. Even if you don't

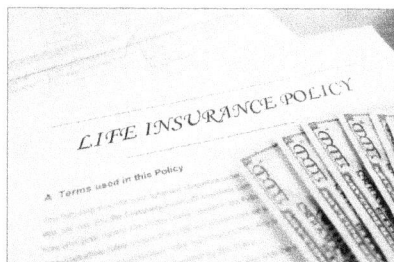

care about replacing the money borrowed from the policy, you will owe annual interest on the loan. If you don't pay back the interest, the interest will start to compound—your loved one will end up paying interest on their interest.

- ☐ **Surrender.** Your loved one can cancel their policy and gain a large amount of cash from the surrender. Drawbacks of surrendering a policy include potentially hefty surrender fees, income taxation, and loss of the policy's death benefit. In addition, a large cash inflow may cause your loved one to become ineligible for Medicaid and Medicare supplemental plans such as Extra Help and Medicare Savings Programs.

- ☐ **Viatical (life) settlement.** In this situation, the company that provides the viatical settlement buys the insurance policy in exchange for monthly, tax-free cash payments. This option is generally reserved for people with a life expectancy of five years or fewer. When your loved one makes a viatical settlement, the company becomes the beneficiary of the insurance policy. Your loved one's original beneficiaries, such as their spouse or children, will not be paid upon your loved one's death.

Personal Finances

All medical and non-medical expenses that are not covered by private or public health insurance will need to be paid out of your loved one's personal finances. These finances include any form of income, such as retirement accounts, Social Security, or veteran's benefits, and any form of savings, including cash accounts and investments. The following sections will describe each of these types of income and savings.

Personal Wealth

If your loved one has designated you as their durable power of attorney for finances, you will need to understand your loved one's personal finances in order to pay for medical or other bills that are not covered by insurance. If you are your loved one's durable power of attorney for healthcare and/or their full-time caregiver, you may also find it helpful to understand your loved one's financial resources so you understand what services your loved one is eligible for and can afford. By understanding your loved one's resources, you can make sure their bills are paid while protecting their assets as much as possible.

Checklist: Financial resources that can help your loved one pay for care

☐ **Cash accounts.** Checking accounts, savings accounts, certificates of deposit, money market accounts, and other cash accounts can help pay medical and non-medical expenses. Many cash accounts provide minimal interest.

☐ **Retirement plans.** Former employers' pension plans or personal retirement accounts may provide a regular source of income.

☐ **Investments.** Investments in bonds, stocks, and mutual funds can provide your loved one with a steady or lump-sum source of income. Income can be in the form of interest, dividends, or the sale price of the investment. Other types of investments are available, but they are for more advanced investors. If your loved one has more complex investments, you will likely need to discuss your loved one's investment portfolio with a professional financial advisor or investment banker.

☐ **Social Security.** Social Security retirement benefits, disability benefits, and Supplemental Security Income (SSI) provide monthly income for many individuals with Alzheimer's disease.

☐ **Veterans Benefits.** If your loved one was in the armed services, they can receive a range of benefits from the U.S. Department of Veterans Affairs.

☐ **Annuities.** An annuity is a contractual financial investment purchased through an insurance company to provide a steady source of income for either a set period of time or for the rest of your loved one's life. If your loved one purchased a fixed annuity, the amount of each payment will never vary. If they purchased a variable annuity, the amount of each payment will vary with the value of the annuity's underlying investments. Annuities often have high expenses and large penalties for early withdrawal, so make sure you

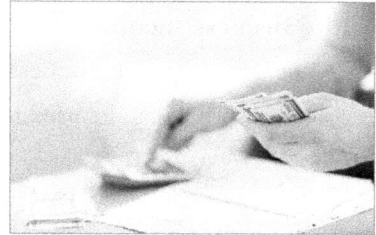

and your loved one understand the rules and regulations associated with the annuity before purchase.

☐ **Rental income.** If your loved one owns property that they rent or lease, rent payments provide a reliable income stream.

☐ **Business income.** If your loved one owns a business, they may be receiving income from the business, or they may sell the business to obtain a lump sum of cash that can be used to pay expenses.

☐ **Personal property.** Alternative investments such as real estate, vehicles, jewelry, art, or collectibles can be liquidated to cover care costs.

☐ **Trusts.** Your loved one may be the beneficiary of a trust set up by their parents, grandparents, or spouse. Any income or resources from the trust can be used to help pay for medical or non-medical expenses according to the trust's stipulations.

In the event of a terminal illness like Alzheimer's disease, both medical and non-medical expenses can greatly erode your loved one's wealth. You and your loved one may choose to spend all of your loved one's assets to pay for their care and qualify for Medicaid. However, if your loved one wishes to protect their savings and resources for their descendants' inheritance, the techniques in the checklist below may be beneficial.

Checklist: How to protect your loved one's finances

☐ Talk to a qualified financial advisor or elder law attorney for legal advice about protecting your loved one's finances. This should be done as soon as possible while your loved one still has the ability to make competent decisions.

☐ Create a durable power of attorney for finances to name a trusted person or group of people to make financial decisions for your loved one while they are alive. This helps protect your loved one from unnecessary spending and scams when they no longer have the mental capacity to make good financial decisions. Your loved one must choose their own power of attorney and be legally competent to sign documents, so this should also be done as soon as possible.

☐ Be aware of common financial scams and types of identity theft, and take action to prevent your loved one from becoming a target.

☐ Limit marketing materials that come to your loved one's home so that they are not tempted to make out-of-the-ordinary, expensive, or unnecessary purchases. Similarly, post a "No Soliciting" sign on your loved one's door.

☐ Organize and protect your loved one's financial documents by knowing where bank, Social Security, pension, and personal papers are. Store your loved one's impossible-to-replace documents, including birth certificates, property deeds, and vehicle titles, in a safe place. If you store them at home, keep these documents in a fireproof and waterproof container. If you store them in a safe deposit box, make sure the durable power of attorney for finances is listed as a co-signee on the box.

☐ Make and stick to a budget. With the added expense of paying for care, a budget is essential for managing the finances of a person with Alzheimer's disease.

☐ Pay bills on time to avoid the late fees associated with nonpayment.

☐ Use credit cards cautiously, because credit card debt comes with high interest rates and can be difficult to repay. Ideally, you should only use a credit card if you can completely pay off the balance each month to avoid interest and late fees.

☐ Review your loved one's credit reports for errors. Having an error-free credit report can make buying insurance and borrowing money substantially easier.

☐ If your loved one is paying for banking services, consider switching their accounts to a bank with no account fees.

☐ Consider switching to online banking and bill paying to prevent mistakes and save money. You'll have access to more information if you bank electronically, and you'll be able to schedule payments automatically and monitor account balances in real time.

☐ If your loved one has trouble spending money wisely but insists on having a checkbook, bank card, or credit card, talk to the bank or credit institution to set up a method to protect against overdraft charges and large credit card bills. Banks often allow linking of checking and savings accounts to prevent overdraft fees, and setting a low spending limit on credit cards can help prevent large bills.

☐ Resist the urge to borrow an "advance" on your loved one's future pension, Social Security, or other retirement income. Borrowing from these sources generally involve costly fees and interest.

☐ If possible, don't make early withdrawals from term accounts, because doing so can lead to costly fees. These accounts include certificates of deposit (CDs), certain investments, and retirement accounts.

☐ Do not sell your loved one's primary home, especially if a spouse, child under age 21, adult child with a disability, or caregiver sibling is still living there. An individual's primary residence is exempt from Medicaid asset requirements. If your loved one sells their home and has a windfall of cash, it may cause them to lose eligibility for Medicaid and other programs with asset restrictions. For more information, see Checklist: How to protect your loved one's home.

☐ Avoid a reverse mortgage if possible. A reverse mortgage is essentially a loan with your loved one's house as collateral. The money is paid to your loved one in monthly cash payments that can be used for your loved one's care and living expenses. Upon your loved one's death, the bank sells the house to recover their investment.

☐ When applying for Medicaid for nursing home care benefits, invoke the spousal impoverishment provisions if your loved one's spouse is still living in the community.

☐ If possible, purchase long-term care insurance through a state Partnership program. This allows your loved one to protect their assets up to the amount of their insurance benefits.

☐ Prepare for the transfer of financial responsibility and assets by communicating with your loved one about relevant financial documents and the structure of their finances.

☐ Determine a method of transferring wealth before your loved one is no longer capable of making financial decisions. Typical ways to transfer wealth include gifting assets, selling possessions for a reduced price, and paying for a family member to provide care services.

☐ If your loved one wants to transfer wealth by gifting assets or selling them for less than their market value, they should do this as soon as possible. If they gift assets within five years of needing Medicaid to help pay for long-term nursing care, they will be penalized. However, if they give away assets early so the gifts are beyond the look-back period, they will not be penalized by Medicaid. Large gifts may incur gift taxes, so consider the effect of taxes on your loved one and the recipient before giving cash or other assets as a gift.

☐ If a family member is providing caregiving services for your loved one, consider drawing up a caregiver payment agreement to pay the individual for their caregiving services. This may be especially helpful for the family member if they had to quit their job to provide caregiving services for your loved one. Paying a family member for caregiving services helps legitimately transfer wealth and spend down your loved one's assets without incurring a Medicaid penalty. However, make sure your loved one and the family member draw up a written, legal agreement to prove to Medicaid that the payments are legitimate. Remember that the family member will be required to pay income taxes on this money, similar to a regular job.

☐ Consider establishing a trust as a way of transferring wealth. In particular, an irrevocable trust can be established for your loved one's life insurance policy to ensure that the beneficiaries receive payment after your loved one's death. An irrevocable trust is no longer considered the possession of the individual but rather of the beneficiaries. Other types of trusts may also be beneficial.

☐ Establish a will for the orderly distribution of assets upon your loved one's death. If a will is not established, state law determines how assets will be distributed. Meet with an attorney to draft a will that reflects your loved one's goals.

Depending on your loved one's need for Medicaid, their estate—in particular, their home—may be subject to the Medicaid Estate Recovery process. To protect your loved one's home from recovery, consider taking the steps in the checklist below. Realize, however, that some states have different recovery rules that may allow Medicaid to recover your loved one's home regardless of any legal documents allowing heirs to inherit the home.

Checklist: How to protect your loved one's home

Establishing a life estate:

☐ A life estate is a form of joint property ownership between two or more people.

☐ A life estate has two parties of interest with a claim to the real estate: the life tenant and the remainder tenant.

☐ Life tenants (typically your loved one and/or spouse) have the right to live in the home for the remainder of their life. As such, they have the responsibility to pay mortgage payments, property taxes, home insurance, maintenance costs, etc. just as if they were the sole owner.

☐ Remainder tenants (typically a child or children of the life tenant) gain ownership of the property upon the life tenant's death. If there is more than one life tenant, ownership transfers upon the death of the last remaining life tenant.

☐ With a life estate, the life tenant is not allowed to sell the property to others without the consent of the remainder tenants. If the life tenant sells the property on their own, they can only sell it for the duration of their life. Upon their death, the ownership of the property reverts to the remainder tenants even if the property was sold to a third party by the life tenant.

☐ Remainder tenants are not allowed to displace the life tenants from their home or sell the property without the life tenants' consent, because they have no legal right to the property while the life tenant is still living. Because they have no right to the property while the life tenant is alive, creditors have no claim on the property if the remainder tenants have financial or legal issues.

- [ ] Property in a life estate does not have to go through probate upon the life tenant's death, thus avoiding court fees and potentially recovery through the Medicaid Estate Recovery program, depending on state laws.

- [ ] If the property is placed in a life estate more than five years before the life tenant applies for Medicaid, the transfer of property cannot incur a Medicaid penalty when the life tenant applies to Medicaid for long-term care benefits. Therefore, if your loved one may potentially need Medicaid in the future, it is best to establish the life estate as soon as possible so it falls outside the look-back period.

- [ ] If your loved one needs Medicaid in the near future, they should not establish a life estate, because it will be counted as a gift during the Medicaid look-back period and they will have to wait through the penalty period before Medicaid begins to pay.

- [ ] If your loved one needs Medicaid and it has not been five years since the establishment of the life estate, the remainder tenants can voluntarily revert ownership back to the life tenant to avoid the Medicaid penalty. Remainder tenants are not required by law to revert ownership, so the life tenant should choose remainder tenants who will make choices that benefit the life tenant.

Establishing a trust:

- [ ] Your loved one may also protect their home from Medicaid Estate Recovery by transferring the home to an irrevocable trust.

- [ ] An irrevocable trust is a trust that cannot be changed by the grantor, or the person who created the trust. This means that once their home is placed in the trust, they cannot remove it from the trust without the written consent of the beneficiaries.

- [ ] To place a home in the trust, your loved one will need to use a deed to transfer legal title of the property to the trust. After this, all insurance, property tax, and maintenance should be paid by the trust, so your loved one may need to transfer cash to the trust to pay these bills if the trust does not have other available funds. Make sure that you notify the insurance company of the sale so the proper owner can be named in the insurance documents.

- [ ] If your loved one still owes money on their mortgage, you will need to check the conditions of the mortgage before transferring the title to the trust. Some mortgage companies have a "due on transfer" clause that would require your loved one to pay the remainder of the mortgage at the time the property is transferred to the trust.

- [ ] Putting a home in an irrevocable trust exempts it from estate taxes, but it may be subject to a gift tax. Discuss the tax implications of this move with a qualified tax advisor or estate planner.

- [ ] If your loved one places their home in the irrevocable trust, they still have the right to live in the home until their death, but your loved one should make sure this is stated in the terms of the trust.

- [ ] If your loved one is living in a home that is owned and insured by a trust, they will need to consider purchasing renters insurance to insure the contents of the home (their personal possessions).

- [ ] Unlike a revocable trust, the grantor is not allowed to be the trustee of an irrevocable trust (i.e., they cannot manage the trust). In addition, to prevent the assets of the trust from being counted as assets for Medicaid purposes, your loved one and their spouse should not be listed as beneficiaries of the trust.

- [ ] Placing a home in an irrevocable trust protects it from claims against creditors. For example, if your loved one needs Medicaid coverage for long-term care services, Medicaid cannot place a lien on your loved one's home. In addition, they cannot claim the house after your loved one's death because the home is no longer part of your loved one's estate.

- [ ] Similar to the life estate, if your loved one places their home in the irrevocable trust within five years of needing to apply for Medicaid, they will face a Medicaid penalty equal to the value of the house plus the value of the cash transferred to pay for insurance and property tax. Unlike the life estate, the irrevocable trust cannot be reversed to prevent the Medicaid penalty. Because the value of homes is generally high, the penalty period will be very long. It is better to wait until after the five-year look-back period is past before applying for Medicaid.

☐ Because the value of the cash or other assets transferred to the trust for insurance and property tax can be counted against your loved one for Medicaid benefits within the five-year look-back period, your loved one should transfer enough money to the trust to cover these expenses for many years. However, depending on the size of the house and level of insurance chosen, the Medicaid penalty for transferring money to the trust to cover these expenses should be fairly short if your loved one transfers money annually.

☐ If your loved one places their home in an irrevocable trust close to the time that it will need to be sold to pay back Medicaid, the formation of the trust may be considered fraudulent, and your loved one may lose their home anyway. If they want to place their home in an irrevocable trust, it should be done as soon as possible.

Knowing how to protect your loved one's assets, including their home, is an important step in helping your loved one manage their finances and pay for their care. However, you will also need to understand the sources of income that may be available to your loved one, including retirement benefits, Social Security, and veteran's benefits.

Retirement Benefits

During your loved one's working life, they probably accrued money in a retirement account of some kind. Generally, your loved one will have established a plan either in conjunction with an employer or as an individual retirement account.

Employers establish qualified plans to provide retirement benefits for their employees, and such plans can take the form of defined benefit plans or defined contribution plans. A defined benefit plan promises a specified monthly benefit at retirement. This monthly benefit lasts for the rest of the individual's life. The amount of the benefit is usually calculated based on the individual's salary and years of service. The two main types of defined benefit plans are pension plans and cash-balance plans.

In comparison, with a defined contribution plan, the employee or the employer (or both) contribute to the employee's individual account under the plan. Contributions are invested on the employee's behalf, and the employee ultimately receives the balance in their account at retirement. The value of these plans is not set but can increase or decrease depending on changes in the value of the underlying investments. The most common types of defined contribution plans include 401(k)s and 403(b)s.

Individual retirement accounts (IRAs) are opened with financial institutions. Several types of IRAs exist, including traditional IRAs and Roth IRAs, each with their own tax implications and rules regulating use. Although IRAs are not necessarily linked with an employer, they can be a valuable source of income for a person with Alzheimer's disease.

Your loved one may have worked at several institutions over the course of their career, so be sure to check with all of their former employers (and their spouse's former employers) for any forgotten retirement plans.

Checklist: Basics about defined benefit plans

General:

☐ Defined benefit plans are typically funded by the employer, not the employee, and the employer retains the investment risk associated with the plan.

☐ The amount of the retirement payouts to employees is usually based on the employee's salary and years of service, but the formula used to calculate benefits differs with different types of plans.

☐ The two types of defined benefit plans are pension plans and cash-balance plans.

☐ The benefits in most defined benefit plans are protected by federal insurance provided through the Pension Benefit Guaranty Corporation (PBGC).

Pensions:

☐ Pension plans were designed to benefit employees who stayed with one employer for their entire career, with benefits increasing substantially the closer they get to retirement.

- ☐ Pensions promise a regular monthly benefit for the rest of the employee's life after they retire. The amount of this benefit is usually determined based on the employee's years of service, salary, and other factors, but it can also be simply a defined dollar amount.

- ☐ For most pensions, the monthly benefit is based on the employee's average salary over the last five years of employment before retirement rather than their average career salary, thus increasing retirement benefits as the employee's salary increases.

- ☐ Pension plans were much more common several decades ago, so if your loved one worked at the same company for many years, they may have a pension plan through their employer.

- ☐ Pensions are sometimes portable and insured, so it's possible that your loved one has a forgotten pension from a company that no longer exists or that employed them many years ago. Tracking down lost pensions can be difficult but financially rewarding.

- ☐ Pensions can be paid to a surviving spouse in some circumstances, so if your loved one is a widow or widower, you may want to investigate their late spouse's retirement benefits to determine whether they can access any remaining retirement funds.

Cash-balance plans:

- ☐ Cash-balance plans function much like regular pension plans, but with a few elements borrowed from defined contribution plans.

- ☐ In a cash-balance plan, your loved one's retirement benefits are based on a percentage of their salary plus calculated interest over the life of their employment. This amount is recorded in a hypothetical account. For example, the account balance increases by an amount equal to 6% of your loved one's salary each year, plus 5% interest on the previous year's account balance. The interest amount is usually based on the current interest gained from investing in one-year Treasury bills.

☐ When your loved one retires or leaves the company, they are entitled to the balance of their hypothetical account. With these funds, they can either purchase an annuity equal to the balance of the account, or they can receive a lump sum equal to the balance of the account.

☐ If they purchase the annuity, they will receive monthly benefits for the rest of their life after retirement similar to a typical pension plan. The amount of the benefits will depend on the value of the annuity, the number of years until your loved one begins to draw on the annuity, and whether the annuity has fixed or variable payments.

☐ If your loved one elects to receive a lump sum, this money can usually be rolled over into an IRA or other retirement fund.

Checklist: Basics about defined contribution plans

General:

☐ For most defined contribution plans, the employee decides how much they want to contribute to their retirement account. These funds are deducted directly from their paycheck and transferred to their retirement account. Thus, the employee is the main contributor to defined contribution plans.

☐ Most companies also contribute to the employee's retirement account based on company limits, the employee's contribution amounts, and the employee's salary. Many companies will match the employee's contribution up to a certain percentage of the employee's salary.

☐ Employers typically use a technique called "vesting" so that their matched funds are not available until an employee has worked for the company for a specified number of years (usually three or four).

☐ Typically, the employer hires an investment firm to invest the contributions and manage the accounts. The investment firm then provides participating employees with the option of investing in one or more mutual funds based on their investment strategies.

☐ The risks and rewards associated with the plan investments rest completely on the employee rather than the employer, but the employee also has more control over their investment decisions.

401(k) plans:

☐ The annual limit for 401(k) contributions in 2015 is $18,000 for those under age 50 and $24,000 for those age 50 and older.

☐ Funds in a 401(k) account, including earnings after deposit, are taxed when they are withdrawn during retirement, not when they are deposited.

☐ If an employee withdraws money from their 401(k) before the age of 59 ½, the withdrawal will be assessed a 10% penalty, plus regular taxation. However, this penalty can be waived if the money is used to treat a sudden disability or prevent home foreclosure.

☐ After the employee turns 70 ½, they must make required minimum withdrawals from the account.

☐ Certain 401(k) plans also offer shares of the employer's stock.

Roth 401(k) plans:

☐ Roth 401(k) plans are similar to traditional 401(k) plans, except that funds are taxed at the time of contribution rather than the time of withdrawal.

☐ Roth 401(k) accounts are beneficial for individuals who believe they will be in a higher tax bracket after retirement than when the funds are contributed and for those who have many years to let their contributions grow. Because of this, Roth 401(k) accounts are usually most beneficial to younger individuals.

☐ Roth 401(k) plans are relatively new (began in 2006), so your loved one may not have a retirement plan of this type.

☐ Individuals can contribute to a Roth 401(k) up to the same limit as the traditional 401(k), but the sum total deposited in 401(k) and Roth 401(k) accounts cannot be greater than the limit. For example, an individual under the age of 50 could deposit $18,000 in a traditional 401(k) account OR in a Roth 401(k) account, but not both. However, if desired, they could split the $18,000 between the two types of retirement accounts.

☐ In contrast to Roth IRA accounts, anyone, regardless of their income, can contribute to a Roth 401(k) account if it is offered by their employer.

- [ ] If an employee chooses to contribute to a Roth 401(k) account, any employer matching funds will still be deposited in a traditional 401(k) account.

- [ ] Once money is deposited in a Roth 401(k) account, it can never be reverted to a traditional 401(k) account.

- [ ] If your loved one waits until they are 59 ½ to make withdrawals from their Roth 401(k) plan, and if they have participated in the plan for a minimum of five years, all funds withdrawn from the account are tax-free, including earnings.

- [ ] If desired, employees can roll over their Roth 401(k) account to a Roth IRA account when their employment terminates.

- [ ] If the plan permits, your loved one may be able to take a loan from their Roth 401(k) account. The maximum amount of the loan and the repayment plan are usually specified in the plan's rules and guidelines.

403(b) plans:

- [ ] These plans are nearly identical to 401(k) plans, except they are only offered to certain employees of public schools, colleges, and universities; tax-exempt organizations such as charities and some hospitals; and some ministers.

- [ ] Contributions to a 403(b) account can be placed in an annuity through an insurance company, a custodial account invested in mutual funds, or a retirement income account for church employees. These choices are usually more limited than with a 401(k) plan.

- [ ] Employer matching funds may be vested more quickly in 403(b) plans than in similar 401(k) plans.

- [ ] Your loved one may be able to withdraw money from their 403(b) account without penalty before age 59 ½ if they have a financial hardship. Each plan has a different definition of financial hardship, so check with your loved one's plan to determine if any penalties would apply for early withdrawal.

- [ ] These plans are also sometimes offered in a Roth form, where funds are taxed at the time of contribution rather than the time of withdrawal.

457(b) plans:

☐ These plans are also similar to 401(k) plans, except they are only available to state and local government employees, as well as employees of certain tax-exempt organizations.

☐ If an employer offers both a 457(b) plan and a 401(k) plan, employees can invest in both, and therefore potentially double their retirement contribution for the year.

☐ In the three years prior to retirement, individuals can contribute either twice the normal limit or an amount equal to the underutilized limit in previous years, whichever is less, as a special catch-up contribution if the plan allows it.

☐ There are no penalties for making early withdrawals from a 457(b) plan. However, all withdrawals, regardless of age, are still subject to regular income taxation.

☐ A Roth form is available for 457(b) plans. Similar to other Roth plans, funds are taxed at the time of contribution rather than at withdrawal.

Thrift savings plans:

☐ These plans are similar to 401(k) plans, except they are only available to employees of the U.S. government, including the armed services.

☐ The thrift savings plan allows employees to invest in six different funds: government security fund, fixed-income fund, common stock fund, small cap stock fund, international stock fund, and life cycle fund.

☐ Money can be transferred to a thrift savings plan from another retirement account upon enrollment in the federal service, and money can be transferred from the thrift savings plan to another retirement account when your loved one leaves the federal service.

☐ Individuals who are deployed in a tax-exempt designated combat zone are allowed to contribute more to their thrift savings plan than other employees, up to $53,000 in 2015.

- [ ] As of 2012, thrift savings plans now have a Roth option, in which contributions are taxed rather than withdrawals. This allows earnings to grow tax free.

- [ ] Individuals who are deployed in a tax-exempt designated combat zone are allowed to contribute tax-exempt earnings to the Roth thrift savings plan, allowing them to never pay taxes on those contributions. However, the Roth funds are limited to the normal $18,000 per year contribution for individuals under the age of 50.

- [ ] For more about thrift savings plans, see the Thrift Savings Plan website.

Employee stock ownership plans (ESOPs):

- [ ] In an ESOP, the company sets up a trust fund with either cash or shares of company stock, and each employee receives shares of stock as compensation.

- [ ] The shares are held in the trust fund and distributed to employees when they retire or leave the company. At that time, the employee can either sell the shares on the open market (for public companies) or sell them back to the company for cash (for public or private companies).

- [ ] Employees must work for the company for a specific number of years to be "vested" in the plan before they are eligible to receive their shares of stock.

Profit-sharing and stock bonus plans:

- [ ] In a profit-sharing plan, the company contributes money from their profits to a trust. The trustee then manages the investments in the trust, and employees are listed as beneficiaries of the trust.

- [ ] Companies must allow all employees to participate in the profit-sharing plan. They cannot favor managers and higher-level employees and exclude lower-level employees.

- [ ] Contributions to the profit-sharing plan are entirely from the employer and not the employee. The employer can determine each year what portion of the company's profits will be contributed to the plan. However, employers are not required to make a contribution.

☐ Profit-sharing plans use a formula that allocates a portion of each annual contribution to each employee. Employers are allowed to contribute up to 25% of each employee's compensation or up to $53,000, whichever is less.

☐ Stock bonus plans are similar to profit-sharing plans except employees have the right to demand their distribution be in shares of company stock rather than in cash.

☐ Profit-sharing and stock bonus plans may also incorporate a 401(k) plan.

Money purchase plans:

☐ Money purchase plans are similar to profit-sharing plans, except the employer is required to contribute to the plan each year.

☐ The employer is required to contribute an amount equal to a certain percentage of the employee's salary—5%, for example—every year.

☐ Unlike profit-sharing plans, both employers and employees are allowed to contribute to a money purchase plan.

☐ Contributions are invested for the employee, and each employee's retirement benefit is based on the value of the contributions to their account and the gains or losses the account has experienced.

Checklist: Individual retirement arrangements (IRAs)

General:

☐ IRAs are retirement accounts that individuals, self-employed persons, and small businesses open with banks.

☐ There are four main types of IRAs: traditional IRAs, Roth IRAs, SEP IRAs, and SIMPLE IRAs.

☐ IRAs can hold a variety of investments, including stocks, bonds, and mutual funds.

☐ Contribution limits for traditional and Roth IRAs combined are $5,500 for individuals under age 50 and $6,500 for individuals age 50 and over.

☐ Individuals can contribute to IRAs even if they contribute to a retirement account at their place of employment.

☐ IRAs cannot be jointly owned, but the amount left in the IRA after the owner's death can be paid to a beneficiary.

Traditional IRAs:

☐ Similar to 401(k) plans, individuals are taxed on distributions or withdrawals from a traditional IRA rather than their contributions. Therefore, earnings on the contributions are also taxed at the time of withdrawal. Distributions must be included in the individual's income tax return for the year of withdrawal.

☐ Although contributions to an IRA may be tax-deductible, individuals with higher income who are also covered by a retirement plan at work may not be able to take a full deduction.

☐ Individuals can contribute to a traditional IRA if they earn taxable income and are under age 70 ½. Individuals over age 70 ½ cannot contribute to a traditional IRA.

☐ Individuals who are under the age of 59 ½ and want to withdraw funds from their traditional IRA will be charged an early withdrawal fee of 10%. However, this penalty may be waived if the distribution is needed to pay unreimbursed medical expenses, if the owner of the account has a disability, or for other qualifying reasons.

☐ Individuals who are between the age of 59 ½ and 70 ½ can withdraw funds from traditional IRAs with no penalty, and they can withdraw any amount.

☐ Individuals who are age 70 ½ or older must begin withdrawing required minimum annual distributions. The minimum distribution can be calculated using a worksheet supplied by the IRS. This amount may change every year, so make sure this calculation is done correctly. Individuals may withdraw any amount, as long as it exceeds the required minimum. If the amount is less than the required minimal distribution, your loved one will pay a 50% excise tax on the portion of the money that was not distributed as required.

Roth IRAs:

☐ Roth IRAs are similar to traditional IRAs except that contributions to these accounts are taxed, whereas withdrawals are not. Earnings are allowed to grow tax-free.

- Individuals with a high income are not allowed to contribute to a Roth IRA. For example, in 2015, single individuals with income higher than $131,000 and married individuals filing jointly with income higher than $193,000 cannot contribute to a Roth IRA.

- As long as income requirements are met, any adult can contribute to a Roth IRA at any time, regardless of age. Even individuals older than 70 ½ can continue to contribute to a Roth IRA.

- Many types of retirement plans can be rolled over into a Roth IRA account, but the amount rolled over will be taxable if it came from a non-Roth account. For example, money rolled over from a 401(k) account would be taxed upon rollover, but money from a Roth 401(k) account would not be taxed.

- Individuals who are under the age of 59 ½ and want to withdraw funds from their traditional IRA can withdraw their original contributions with no penalty if the account has been open for at least five years. If they withdraw earnings before the age of 59 ½, they will be subject to a 10% early withdrawal fee, and the earnings will be taxed.

- Individuals who are over the age of 59 ½ can withdraw any amount at any time with no penalty, as long as the account has been open for at least five years. Both original contributions and earnings can be withdrawn tax-free.

- In contrast to traditional IRAs, individuals are not required to take minimum distributions from Roth IRAs at age 70 ½. The money can remain in the account untouched to be passed on to the next generation if desired.

SEP IRAs:

- SEP IRAs are most commonly used by small business owners or self-employed individuals. However, a business of any size can open a SEP IRA as long as they do not offer any other type of retirement account.

- SEP IRAs are usually combined with the individual's traditional IRA as one account. The SEP IRA portion of the account is for contributions made by the employer, and the traditional IRA portion of the account is for contributions made by the employee. Employees are not allowed to contribute to SEP IRAs.

☐ The employer can contribute an amount up to 25% of the employee's compensation or $53,000, whichever is less. Employers can decide how much they want to contribute within this limit, and the contribution amount may change for each period depending on the financial state of the company. Catch-up contributions are not allowed in SEP IRAs.

☐ The limits for contribution to a SEP IRA account and a traditional IRA account do not affect each other. Both the employer and the employee can maximize their contributions based on federal laws. However, participation in an employer-funded SEP IRA may reduce the tax deduction that the employee can take for their traditional IRA contributions.

☐ As with a traditional IRA, funds are taxed at the time of withdrawal. Employees do not pay taxes at the time of contribution.

☐ Distribution rules and penalties are the same as for traditional IRAs.

SIMPLE IRAs:

☐ Savings Incentive Match Plan for Employees (SIMPLE) IRAs are intended for small business (fewer than 100 employees) and self-employed individuals. The employer is not allowed to offer any other retirement plan if they provide a SIMPLE IRA.

☐ As with a traditional IRA, funds are taxed at the time of withdrawal rather than at the time of contribution.

☐ These accounts are much like SEP IRAs, except that employees can make contributions. Employees are allowed to contribute up to $12,500 to their SIMPLE IRA account in 2015. Individuals age 50 or over can make catch-up contributions up to $3,000 in 2015.

☐ In SIMPLE IRAs, employers are required to contribute to their employees' SIMPLE IRAs using either matching or nonelective contributions.

☐ With matching contributions, employers contribute a dollar-for-dollar matching contribution up to 3% of the employee's salary. Employees that do not contribute do not receive matching funds that year. The percentage the employer matches can be lower than 3% in two out of every five years.

☐ With nonelective contributions, the employer contributes a flat 2% of the employee's compensation, regardless of whether the employee contributes.

☐ Participation in a SIMPLE IRA does not prevent your loved one from participating in a traditional or Roth IRA.

☐ Distribution rules and penalties are the same as for traditional IRAs, except if your loved one withdraws money within the first two years of the account opening and they are under age 59 ½, they will be charged a 25% penalty.

Once you have determined which types of retirement accounts your loved one has and what withdrawal stipulations each account follows, you will need to collect benefits from the retirement accounts to help pay your loved one's medical and other bills. The checklist below describes information that you will need to have on hand in order to begin collecting retirement income on your loved one's behalf.

Checklist: Information needed to receive retirement benefits

☐ Name

☐ Contact information

☐ Date of birth, with birth certificate

☐ Marital status, with marriage certificate

☐ Spouse's date of birth, with birth certificate

☐ Social Security number

☐ Type of benefit being sought

☐ Retirement account information

☐ Retirement date

If your loved one has multiple types of retirement accounts, consider talking to a qualified financial advisor or accountant to make sure your loved one is meeting all the requirements for minimum distributions. If your loved one is under the age of 59 ½ and they need to take distributions from their retirement accounts to cover expenses, a financial advisor or accountant can also walk you through the fees and penalties that may be associated with that withdrawal and help you determine if your loved one qualifies for withdrawal without penalty.

Government Assistance

If your loved one was employed in a Social Security-eligible job or if they have low income, they may be eligible for government assistance to help pay for medical and non-medical expenses. Government programs that provide assistance include Social Security and SNAP (Supplemental Nutrition Assistance Program).

Social Security

If your loved one with Alzheimer's disease was employed (and therefore paid Social Security taxes), they likely qualify for income benefits from the Social Security Administration (SSA), even if they are not yet full retirement age. Social Security (SS) benefits come in three forms: retirement benefits, disability benefits, and supplemental security income (SSI).

Checklist: Basics about Social Security retirement benefits

- ☐ During the years your loved one worked and paid SS taxes, they earned "credits" toward SS benefits. To qualify for SS retirement benefits, your loved one needs 40 credits. One credit is received each quarter SS taxes are paid, which equals 10 years of work before your loved one qualifies for SS benefits.

- ☐ Your loved one's benefit payment is based on how much they earned during their working career. Higher lifetime earnings result in higher benefits. You can estimate your loved one's benefit level online using the SSA Retirement Estimator.

- ☐ Your loved one can get SS retirement benefits as early as age 62. However, they will receive a reduced benefit if they retire before the full retirement age. Your loved one can delay their retirement payments up to age 70 if desired.

☐ If your loved one was born in 1948 or earlier, they are already eligible for a full SS benefit. If your loved one was born between 1949 and 1954, they will be eligible for full SS benefits at the age of 66. If your loved one was born between 1955 and 1960, the age at which full retirement benefits are payable increases gradually to age 67. Individuals born after 1960 are eligible for full benefits at the age of 67.

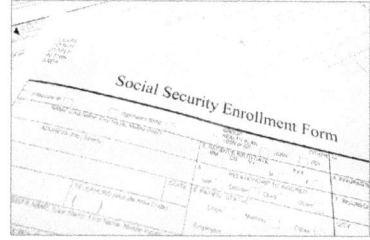

☐ If your loved one is able to continue working past their full retirement age, they will increase their SS benefit upon retirement both because they had higher lifetime earnings and because SS increases their benefit by a certain percentage each year they don't claim retirement benefits.

☐ Widows and widowers can begin receiving SS benefits at age 60, or at age 50 if they have a disability and the disability started before or within 7 years of their spouse's death. If desired, the widow or widower can take reduced benefits on their late spouse's account until they reach full retirement age and then switch their benefits to their own account to start receiving full benefits.

☐ If your loved one is eligible to receive full retirement benefits, sometimes their other family members, specifically their spouse and minor or disabled children, can also receive benefits, including spouses who are age 62 or older; former spouses who are 62 or older; spouses who are younger than 62, if they are taking care of a child entitled on the retiree's record who is younger than age 16 or has a disability; children up to age 18 (or 19 if they have not yet graduated from high school); and children of any age with a disability.

☐ Some individuals who receive SS retirement benefits have to pay taxes on those benefits. Talk to a trusted tax advisor or accountant to determine if your loved one will need to pay taxes.

☐ Your loved one can apply for retirement benefits online, or they can call the agency at 1-800-772-1213. They can also apply in person at any SS office. Certain information is required for enrollment, including the applicant's SS number, birth certificate, W-2 forms, and other documents.

If your loved one has to retire early because of Alzheimer's disease and they are not yet eligible to receive SS retirement benefits, they should consider applying for SS disability benefits. The amount of the disability benefit is the same as a full, unreduced retirement benefit. In my dad's case, he was diagnosed at age 62, so we had to apply for disability. The process took several months and (in his case) was not retroactive, so there were months when he was disabled but did not receive disability income. Therefore, it is best to apply as early as possible once your loved one meets the disability requirements.

Checklist: Basics about Social Security disability benefits

☐ Disability benefits are for individuals under age 65 who have been employed for a specified time, now have a disability, and are not currently receiving SS benefits. SS only pays for total disability, not partial disability.

☐ To meet employment requirements, your loved one must meet both a recent work requirement and a duration of work requirement. To meet the recent work requirement, individuals over the age of 31 must have worked at least five years out of the 10-year period before their disability began. To meet the duration of work requirement, individuals age 28 must have worked at least 1.5 years, and that duration increases by 0.5 years for every two years of age.

☐ Your loved one must also meet Social Security's very strict definition of disability. Your loved one is considered disabled under SS rules if (1) they cannot do work they did before; (2) they cannot adjust to other work because of their medical condition(s); and (3) their disability has lasted or is expected to last for at least one year or to result in death.

☐ To help meet the disability requirements, your loved one must provide proof of their diagnosis of and treatment for Alzheimer's disease.

☐ Before your loved one applies for SS disability, they should print and review the Adult Disability Checklist online. This checklist details the documents needed to apply for and receive disability benefits.

☐ Even if your loved one does not have all the necessary documents listed in the checklist, don't delay in applying for disability benefits. SS will help them get whatever documents they need.

☐ To begin the disability application, fill out the Disability Benefit Application and the Medical Release Form online. You can also apply by phone at 1-800-772-1213 or in person by making an appointment at your local SS office.

☐ SS welcomes those who wish to help another person apply for disability. When you fill out your loved one's application, SS may ask for information about you, your relationship to the person you are applying for and, if applicable, the organization you work for.

☐ You do not need to be the appointed representative of the person you are helping in order to help them apply for benefits. However, it is important that the person you are helping signs the application, not you.

☐ After your loved one applies for disability, SS will provide confirmation of the application; review the application; contact you if the agency needs more information; inform you if other family members may be able to receive benefits on the applicant's record or if the applicant may be able to receive benefits on another person's record (such as a spouse or loved one); process the application; and mail their decision. This process usually takes a minimum of three to five months.

☐ Payments usually begin within a few months of the disability. The SSA requires a five-month waiting period before disability benefits can begin, so the first SS benefit will be paid for the sixth full month after the disability began. Payments are issued in the month after they are due. For example, your loved one will receive their January disability check in February.

☐ Your loved one may also be eligible for back payments. Back payments allow your loved one to be paid benefits for the months they were waiting for their application to be processed, assuming they are approved for disability benefits. The SSA will not pay for the first five months, but if your loved one's application took longer than five months to process, they may be eligible for back payments during the remaining months of the application process.

- [ ] If your loved one has had a disability for many months before they submit their disability application, they may also be eligible for retroactive payments. If your loved one can establish that the onset date of their disability was prior to their application date, the SSA may pay them for as many as 17 months (one year plus the five-month waiting period) of disability benefits up to their onset date once their application is approved.

- [ ] Like SS retirement benefits, the monthly disability benefit is based on your loved one's lifetime earnings. Therefore, the disability benefit will be different for each person. In addition, your loved one may have to pay taxes on the benefits they receive similar to SS retirement benefits.

- [ ] The SSA requires electronic transfer of funds, so you will want to set up electronic payments for your loved one.

- [ ] If your loved one is unable to handle their own money, the SSA can send the benefit payments to another responsible individual who promises to use the funds to care for your loved one. A caregiver or durable power of attorney would be a good choice for receiving these funds on behalf of your loved one, but they must be approved by the SSA. This individual is called a representative payee. The representative payee is responsible for tracking how the money is spent or saved so they can prove that they are using the money to care for the intended individual. Financial reports will need to be filed annually by the representative payee.

- [ ] In general, benefits will continue as long as your loved one is disabled. However, the law requires that the SSA review the case periodically to see whether the person is still disabled. Because your loved one is unlikely to improve, these reviews will likely take place once every five to seven years.

- [ ] Once your loved one reaches full retirement age, they will automatically begin receiving retirement benefits rather than disability benefits. The amount they receive each month should remain the same.

- [ ] Once your loved one receives SS disability benefits for two years, they will automatically be enrolled in Medicare. Your loved one may also be eligible for the Supplemental Nutrition Assistance Program or for Medicaid.

In addition to retirement and disability benefits, SS also has a Supplemental Security Income (SSI) program for individuals who are blind, disabled, or over the age of 65 who meet specific income and asset requirements. The requirements for this program are similar to those for Medicaid assistance, and they are detailed in the following checklist.

Checklist: Basics about Supplemental Security Income (SSI)

- ☐ To determine whether your loved one is eligible for SSI benefits, you can use the Benefit Eligibility Screening Tool online.

- ☐ Income requirements are based off of monthly federal benefit rates. Currently, these rates are $733 for an individual or $1,100 for a couple if they live on their own. Rates are decreased if they live with someone else and do not share housing costs. Countable income is then subtracted from this benefit rate to determine their SSI benefit. For example, a single individual living alone with $300 in countable income would receive an SSI benefit of $433 monthly.

- ☐ Asset or resource limits are $2,000 in countable assets for a single individual and $3,000 in countable assets for a couple. Assets include cash, bank accounts, stocks and bonds, land, vehicles, personal property, life insurance, and other resources that could be converted to cash. However, not all assets are countable assets. For example, your loved one's primary home, household goods and personal items, one vehicle, some burial funds, some life insurance policies, and SS benefits are not included as countable assets.

- ☐ If your loved one qualifies for SSI based on a disability, disability requirements are the same as for the SS disability benefits. In this case, they would be qualified to receive both SS disability and SSI benefits.

- ☐ Similarly, if your loved one is at full retirement age, they are likely eligible for SS retirement benefits. Receiving SS disability or retirement benefits does not exempt them from receiving SSI benefits.

- ☐ Currently, the SSI application is not available online. To apply for benefits for your loved one, you must schedule an appointment with the local SS office.

To make an appointment, call 1-800-772-1213 from 7 a.m. to 7 p.m., Monday through Friday, or contact your local SS office directly.

- ☐ Documents your loved one may need for application include their SS card or number, proof of age (such as a birth certificate), proof of citizenship status, proof of income and resources, work history, medical records, and other documents. For a full list, contact your local SS office when you call to make an appointment.

- ☐ If your loved one is unable to complete the application on their own, they are welcome to appoint a representative who can help them complete the application. To do this, they must complete appropriate forms appointing the representative. This form is different than selecting a representative payee.

Supplemental Nutrition Assistance Program (SNAP)

Low-income individuals and families may be eligible for government assistance with buying groceries through the Supplemental Nutrition Assistance Program, or SNAP (formerly food stamps). SNAP works with state agencies and community resources to provide nutritional information to individuals who receive benefits through SNAP.

Checklist: Basics about SNAP

- ☐ To be eligible for SNAP, your loved one must meet certain income and asset requirements. SNAP provides an online eligibility tool to help determine whether your loved one is eligible for the program.

- ☐ To receive SNAP benefits, your loved one's household must have $2,250 or less in countable resources, or $3,250 or less if at least one person is age 60 or older or has a disability. Countable assets do not include the primary home, and most states do not count one vehicle. Other assets may also be excluded.

- ☐ Income requirements for SNAP are based on either 100% of the federal poverty level for net income or 130% of the federal poverty level for gross income. Because it is based on the federal poverty level, the number of individuals in the household will influence the monthly income allowed.

☐ The allotment received from SNAP will depend on the family's net monthly income and the number of people in the household. The allotment is calculated by subtracting 30% of the family's net income from the maximum allotment for the household size.

☐ To receive SNAP benefits, a member of the household must apply in person at the local state or county office or apply online by visiting the state agency's website. The household must file an application form, have a face-to-face or phone interview, and provide information related to income and expenses. An authorized representative is allowed to complete the application process if an individual from the household cannot complete the application, but the representative must be authorized in writing.

Benefits for Military Personnel and Their Families

The U.S. military and Department of Veterans Affairs (VA) provide numerous programs for military retirees, veterans, and their families. These benefits include both income benefits and health benefits, including access to VA health facilities. The details of these benefits are provided in the checklists below.

Checklist: Income benefits for military personnel

☐ **Retirement pay.** If your loved one was in the military for 20 years or more, they are eligible to receive retirement pay from the military. The military calculates retirement pay depending on the date of enrollment, your loved one's pay while on active duty, and years of service.

☐ **Disability.** Disability payments from the VA are based on the extent of service-related injuries and are not dependent on income. These payments would have begun when the disability was first suffered. Your loved one will likely not qualify for VA disability if they did not sustain a service-related disability.

☐ **Veterans pensions.** Veterans pensions are available to individuals who enlisted before September 7, 1980, who have at least 90 days of active duty service, with at least one day during a wartime period. If the individual enlisted after September 7, 1980, they must have 24 months of active duty service, with at least one day during a wartime period. In addition, they must be age 65 or older, have a disability, be a patient in a nursing home receiving skilled nursing care, or be receiving SS disability or SSI benefits. The individual must also meet income and asset requirements to receive pension benefits.

☐ **Aid and Attendance for veterans.** Aid and Attendance benefits are for veterans who need daily unskilled nursing care at home or in a nursing home. These payments increase the monthly pension benefits. Services that qualify for Aid and Attendance include needing help with activities of daily living such as eating, bathing, and toileting.

☐ **Housebound veterans.** Veterans who are housebound due to a permanent disability, service-related or not, may be eligible for payments in addition to pension payments. However, housebound payments cannot be made to veterans who are receiving Aid and Attendance payments.

Checklist: Health benefits for military personnel

☐ **TRICARE.** If your loved one is an active duty service member or retired from the military, they are eligible to receive health benefits through TRICARE, the military's healthcare program.

☐ **Access to VA facilities.** Eligible veterans with or without disabilities can receive medical services through the VA. Some veterans also receive dental services. Eight different enrollment Priority Groups establish priority for insurance enrollment that vary according to the type of service, extent of disability, and household income. Note that the VA healthcare system is infamous for its long wait times, sloppy recordkeeping, and treatment delays. Before using your loved one's VA benefits, be sure to research local VA facilities and evaluate whether the VA system meets your loved one's needs.

☐ **Armed Forces Retirement Homes.** Some retirees are eligible to live in one of two armed forces retirement homes located in Washington, D.C., and Gulfport, MS. Retirees must be at least 60 years old and must have served for at least 20 years. However, they must be able to live independently at time of admission, so they would have to enter the facility early in the course of Alzheimer's disease. In addition, they cannot have any psychiatric problems, and some individuals with Alzheimer's disease display psychiatric symptoms, so they may be ineligible based on their psychiatric history.

- [ ] **Home and community-based services.** The VA offers multiple home and community-based services for veterans, including adult day healthcare, home-based primary care, homemaker and home health aide care, hospice and palliative care, PACE, respite care, skilled home healthcare, telehealth care, and veteran-directed care. A co-pay may be charged for some of these services, and services may not be available in all areas or for all veterans.

- [ ] **Long-term care options.** The VA offers short- and long-term nursing home benefits through three avenues: VA nursing homes (generally restricted to veterans who were disabled during military service), state nursing homes, and community nursing homes. VA benefits for long-term care will depend on your loved one's eligibility based on their service status, level of disability, and income. In addition, your loved one must be enrolled in the VA standard medical benefits package to be eligible for long-term care benefits.

Checklist: Benefits for families of military personnel

- [ ] **TRICARE.** Eligible current spouses, widows/widowers, dependent parents, and even dependent parents-in-law of active duty or retired military personnel can receive health benefits through TRICARE.

- [ ] **CHAMPVA.** Spouses and children of individuals who are disabled due to a service-connected disability or who had a service-related disability at the time of death may qualify for benefits through the Civilian Health and Medical Program of the VA (CHAMPVA) if they do not qualify for TRICARE. The CHAMPVA program shares medical costs with the policy holder similar to other medical insurance plans. If your loved one is eligible for Medicare, they must be enrolled in Medicare Part A and Part B to be eligible for CHAMPVA.

- [ ] **Pensions for survivors.** Un-remarried spouses and dependent children of deceased wartime veterans who also have limited incomes may be eligible for monthly pension payments. These payments are designed to bring the beneficiary's income up to a certain level, so they vary according to the person's existing income.

- [ ] **Dependency and Indemnity Compensation for survivors.** This program is for the un-remarried spouses and dependent children of veterans who died in the line of duty or who died related to injuries suffered in the line of duty. Parents of individuals who died in the line of duty may also be eligible for indemnity compensation.

- [ ] **Aid and Attendance or Housebound benefits.** Qualified widows, widowers, and dependent children of veterans are eligible to receive Aid and Attendance or Housebound benefits in addition to pension or indemnity payments.

Checklist: Basics about TRICARE

- [ ] TRICARE is a military healthcare program to provide insurance coverage for active duty service members, National Guard and Reserve members, retirees, their families, survivors, former spouses, and others registered in the Defense Enrollment Eligibility Reporting System. The available plans depend on the individual's active duty status.

- [ ] TRICARE offers three basic plans: TRICARE Prime, TRICARE Extra, and TRICARE Standard. They also offer TRICARE for Life, which provides additional coverage for individuals qualified for Medicare (enrollment in Medicare Part A and Part B is required). They also have special plans for National Guard members, retired National Guard members, and their families.

- [ ] Most individuals with Alzheimer's disease who qualify for TRICARE will be retired service members who are over the age of 65 and on Medicare. Therefore, TRICARE for Life will likely be the service plan selected.

- [ ] For individuals eligible to participate in TRICARE for Life, enrollment is not necessary and there are no premiums (however, the individual must still pay Part B premiums). Services covered by Medicare and TRICARE have no annual deductible, and there is a $3,000 catastrophic cap per family per year for covered medical expenses.

- [ ] Through their various plans, TRICARE provides medical and hospital coverage for medically necessary services, prescription coverage, dental services, vision services, preventive services, health screenings, and mental health care.

☐ TRICARE primarily uses military healthcare professionals and facilities for services, but these military healthcare services are supported by civilian services as needed.

☐ For more information about TRICARE, visit the TRICARE website.

If you believe your loved one qualifies for military or veteran's benefits, you should contact their local VA office or visit the VA website.

Community Assistance

Many local community organizations provide low-cost services to people with Alzheimer's disease, such as meal delivery, transportation, and care service facilitation. Each community has a different set of programs, so you may need to do some research into what resources are available in your area.

Checklist: Types of community assistance

☐ Adult day care centers

☐ Advice on financial considerations and assistance

☐ Advice on legal matters

☐ Caregiver support

☐ Counseling and support groups

☐ Crisis intervention

☐ Education workshops

☐ Elder care consulting and advocacy

☐ Housing or rental assistance

☐ Meal assistance

☐ Medical information

☐ Respite care for caregivers

☐ Subsidies for home care

☐ Transportation

☐ Utility assistance

Checklist: How to find low-cost community resources

☐ Search online for your state's Department of Aging, Elder Affairs, or Senior Services. These agencies provide state-specific information and resources.

☐ Search your city's government sites for community resources provided for medically or financially needy individuals.

☐ Search online for charitable organizations in your area that may provide services or resources for people with your loved one's specific needs.

☐ If your loved one is religious, their denomination may offer low-cost services. For example, the Catholic order Little Sisters of the Poor offers nursing home services to the very poorest older people in need of care.

☐ The U.S. Administration on Aging and AARP provide information and low-cost services to millions of older Americans.

☐ Talk to family members, community leaders, friends, faith community members, and others about helping or locating low-cost care options.

☐ The Alzheimer's Association, National Council on Aging, and Eldercare Locator all provide online tools for locating community resources.

Other Considerations

A solid understanding of financial matters is one of the first functions lost by people suffering from Alzheimer's disease, and many of the financial resources available to your loved one can be very confusing even for those without Alzheimer's disease. Therefore, you should begin the process of transitioning control of finances to a durable power of attorney as soon as possible after your loved one's diagnosis. Once you're helping your loved one with their finances, it's important to remember that saving money is almost as important as spending money wisely. Maintaining a clear idea of how your loved one is using money is essential, especially considering that people with Alzheimer's disease are vulnerable to scams. To conserve capital, you—the caregiver—should also be aware of the potential tax implications of spending your own money on Alzheimer's care. Learning the facts now can help you avoid mistakes later in the caregiving process.

Transitioning Control of Finances

Because Alzheimer's disease is progressive, your loved one will be better able to participate in financial decision making early in the course of the disease, and transitioning control of finances will be much simpler if your loved one is able to agree to the changes their financial representative is making. If you wait too long to talk to your loved one, they might put their finances at risk by engaging in erratic spending behaviors, falling prey to scams, and/or failing to make good choices about insurance and medical costs. To add to this urgency, your loved one is only able to sign power of attorney documents while they are still legally competent early in the course of the disease. If your loved one is no longer legally competent, you will have to go to court to be named conservator for your loved one. This process can take months, and your loved one will still be in control of their finances during this time, even if they are making poor financial decisions.

I (Laura) waited too long to take control of my dad's finances. At the time, I lived several states away, and I did not realize how bad my dad's mind was. This was, in part, due to the incorrect medical diagnosis we had received. By the time I had taken control of Dad's finances, this is what he had done:

☐ Given thousands to scammers in Jamaica in hopes of winning a "lottery"

☐ Bought a vacation timeshare

☐ Loaned money to "friends" who we never heard from again

☐ Overpaid credit cards by several hundred dollars, which then had to be refunded

☐ Given thousands to the humane society (I'm all for giving to charity, but this was money he needed, and the humane society was not a cause he would have chosen had he been thinking clearly.)

☐ Made mistakes that cost him bank fees and similar charges

73

I was only able to recover about 20% of the money mentioned above. In trying to recover these funds, I learned that entire networks of people prey on the sick and elderly. They even exchange databases that include names, addresses, and what they personally know about each individual. Law enforcement is overwhelmed with "more important" issues and will not spend much time helping you bring these scammers to justice. In the case of the Jamaican "lottery," I had the phone number, address, and name of the person who contacted my dad. I talked to the U.S. State Department and filled out several forms, but I never heard anything back. Government agencies do not have the funds to track down all the crooks in the world, and the amount of $2,000 was petty to them, even though it was a large amount for my father.

How can you ensure your loved one does not make similar costly financial mistakes? Watch for signs of financial mismanagement, then begin discussing your financial concerns with your loved one as soon as possible so you have ample time to find a financial management strategy that works for your family. The following checklists will help guide you through this process, but you should also talk to a financial planner if you have difficulty working out a solution for your personal situation.

Checklist: Signs your loved one can no longer handle their own finances

- ☐ Your loved one has difficulty counting change, paying for a store purchase, calculating a tip, balancing a checkbook, or understanding a bank statement.

- ☐ Your loved one does not have bills organized.

- ☐ Your loved one pays bills late, overpays, or forgets to pay entirely. These mistakes can result in late fees, interruption of service, and finance charges.

- ☐ Your loved one demonstrates irrational or uncharacteristic spending patterns.

- ☐ Your loved one has trouble determining whether a letter is a bill or junk mail.

- ☐ Your loved one is overwhelmed by the volume and type of mail they receive.

- ☐ Your loved one shows increased vulnerability to fraud and scams.

- ☐ Your loved one has responded favorably to telemarketers.

If your loved one is no longer capable of handling their own finances, you should find a way to discuss sharing financial responsibility, take necessary legal and financial steps, and plan for their future condition. This may be one of the first discussions you have with your loved one about their diagnosis of Alzheimer's disease, so be sure to take the conversation at a pace that is appropriate to your relationship. Keep in mind that your loved one is probably much more frustrated and scared about their current situation than you are, or they may not be able to grasp that there is a problem at all. It's okay to acknowledge that the situation is difficult but that you will make the best of it together. For a complete discussion of legal steps necessary to transition control of finances as well as a list of ways to approach conversations about legal matters, see *Advance Directives, Durable Power of Attorney, Wills, and Other Legal Considerations.*

Checklist: How to approach a discussion about finances with your loved one

- ☐ Start discussions early. Talking about finances is more comfortable when they are a seemingly distant issue, and legal documents needed to transfer financial responsibility are easiest to create when your loved one is legally competent.

- ☐ Ask permission to talk about financial issues, because your loved one might want to avoid the reality that they will eventually no longer have the mental capacity to manage their own finances. However, be firm and have the discussion, because planning is a necessity.

- ☐ Ask your loved one if they have a plan for dealing with the financial impact of the disease.

- ☐ Look for appropriate opportunities to begin a conversation about finances, and follow through with the discussion when the opportunity arises.

- ☐ Use your best judgment about whether to back off or be persistent if your loved one resists the discussion. If you back off, watch for opportunities to raise the issue again.

75

☐ Make sure your loved one knows that you are raising the subject of finances because you care about them and want to reduce their stress.

☐ Tell your loved one that having the discussion now and keeping up an ongoing conversation will save a lot of anxiety for caregivers later. It will also ensure that your loved one's wishes are thoroughly understood and carried out.

☐ Mention that your loved one's attorney, physician, banker, or insurance representative raised the issue that finances can become complicated for people with Alzheimer's disease.

☐ Set a formal "appointment" to discuss financial matters, especially if an opportunity has not arisen. Meet in a private place and make the conversation an event.

☐ Start with a story of someone else's experience, discussing how they wished they would have had a financial plan in place or were thankful that they had such a plan.

☐ Allow your loved one to set the pace of the conversation.

☐ Make sure to listen carefully during the conversation. Listen for clues about your loved one's wishes, and don't turn the conversation into a debate.

☐ Focus on positive aspects of sharing financial responsibility by mentioning that your loved one will no longer have to pay late fees and suffer the inconvenience of dealing with utility companies and the IRS.

☐ Be caring and supportive, and don't try to move too fast or force the issue.

☐ Be conscious and sympathetic of how gender and cultural differences can affect intergenerational relationships, especially when discussing financial management.

☐ If your loved one is not responding to you, see whether a trusted relative or friend will talk to them about finances.

Once you have begun a discussion about finances with your loved one, it is time to start the transition to managing their finances. The following checklist provides information for individuals who have legal control over finances, such as a spouse or durable power of attorney for finances. If you are a caregiver or child of the individual with Alzheimer's disease and are concerned about their financial situation, talk to someone with legal authority to make financial decisions for your loved one.

Checklist: Making the transition to managing your loved one's finances

Spouse:

☐ If your spouse has Alzheimer's disease and they were the primary individual who managed finances for your household, it is usually relatively easy to legally transition control of finances, especially if you normally file taxes jointly.

☐ Discuss with your spouse all the financial accounts that you held either jointly or separately, including bank accounts, investments, and other accounts. Hopefully, you will have done this throughout the course of your marriage, and you may already know this information even without a discussion.

☐ Accounts that you held jointly will need no further action, because you are already listed as an owner on the account and can complete transactions for that account.

☐ If your spouse had separate accounts for which you are not a joint owner, you will need to be assigned co-ownership of the account. This process is relatively straightforward. You and your spouse simply need to go to the bank or other financial institution and have your spouse add you as a co-owner on the account. This usually must be done in person.

☐ If you file taxes separately, you may not want to be listed as a co-owner on any new accounts because it might affect your taxes. In addition, some accounts, such as IRAs, do not allow joint ownership. In these cases, you can become a durable power of attorney or conservator for your spouse. If your loved one receives Social Security benefits, you will need to be designated as their representative payee.

- [ ] If you are power of attorney or conservator for your spouse, you will need to file the legal paperwork with each financial institution with which your spouse has an account for which you are not a joint owner. It is usually best to file these documents in person. Financial institutions often have their own paperwork that you will need to sign in addition to filing the legal documents.

- [ ] If you cannot visit the financial institution in person to file legal documents, you should call and speak to someone who can give you instructions for how to file legal paperwork. That way you will know which documents they need and who to send them to, and if they need to send you additional paperwork to sign, they can get that process started quickly.

- [ ] If your loved one has a joint account with someone other than you (e.g., a minor or adult child, former spouse, or parent), you will need to talk to the joint owner to determine what needs to be done with that account. If the joint owner is not willing to let you manage the account on your spouse's behalf, you may need to relinquish control of the account to the joint owner. However, if you are power of attorney or conservator for your spouse, you already have legal access to the account as long as you file the correct paperwork with the financial institution.

- [ ] If you normally file taxes separately, it may be beneficial to start filing taxes jointly. Many of the government programs that provide financial assistance have much more favorable financial requirements for couples who file taxes jointly compared to those who file taxes separately.

- [ ] Once you have legal access to manage your loved one's financial accounts, you will need to discuss your household budget with your loved one to make sure all bills are paid on time and correctly. This may also include regular charitable donations that you give.

- [ ] Along with managing the budget, you will need to notify any other companies that require your financial information, such as utility companies, credit card companies, and insurance companies, that you will now be managing the account. Again, if you are both already listed as account owners, you will not need to do anything further. However, if you are not listed as an account owner, you will need to provide the company with the new financial information they need.

☐ If your loved one pays bills or manages accounts online, you will need to get login and password information from them so you can continue to manage those accounts. You should do this as soon as possible before your loved one loses the ability to remember the information.

Non-spouse:

☐ Although account co-ownership may be the best option if the individual with Alzheimer's disease is your spouse, it is not usually the best option in other situations. If you are co-owner of your loved one's accounts and you are not a spouse who files taxes jointly, assuming co-ownership of accounts will also force you to assume half of the tax liability for those accounts. This may significantly impact your own financial situation. Therefore, for someone who is not the spouse of the individual with Alzheimer's disease, co-ownership of accounts should be a last resort.

☐ Rather than being listed as a co-owner on accounts, you should draw up legal paperwork to be your loved one's durable power of attorney or conservator. A durable power of attorney document can be drawn up with the help of an attorney before your loved one is legally incompetent, but a conservator must be appointed by the court if your loved one is no longer legally competent.

☐ Some government programs, such as Social Security and the VA, require their own documentation for individuals managing financial resources received from these institutions. Therefore, you will need to file representative payee or VA fiduciary applications with the appropriate agency. When you are approved, make sure you read all documentation thoroughly so you understand your responsibilities.

☐ Once you have the necessary legal paperwork, you will need to contact each financial institution or company with which your loved one has accounts. This includes banks, investment companies, companies that manage retirement funds, credit card companies, utility companies, mortgage companies, insurance companies, and others. This may also include safe deposit boxes and titles to real estate or vehicles. If possible, file the legal paperwork in person and complete any documents that will allow you to have legal control over your loved one's accounts. If filing in person is not possible, call the institution or company to make arrangements to assume control of the account.

☐ If you have legal control of your loved one's finances, you need to sit down with them (and their spouse, if applicable) to discuss their financial wishes. You need to understand their budget; their normal giving, spending and saving patterns; their tax status; their sources of income; their debts; and other financial resources. Your goal should be to manage their finances the same way they would.

☐ If your loved one manages any accounts online, make sure you learn their login and password information so you can continue to manage those accounts. You may also need to change the email address associated with the account or gain access to their email account so you can receive important communications associated with the account.

Taking on financial responsibility for another individual is a big step. You may be overwhelmed with all the different accounts that need to be managed and updated, and understanding your loved one's financial resources and options may be confusing at times. The following checklist will help you discover ways to simplify your loved one's finances. Remember that the initial transfer of responsibility is the most complicated part. Once you have managed your loved one's finances for a few months, it will get easier.

Checklist: Steps to simplify your loved one's finances

☐ Get monthly income sources like Social Security and pension checks directly deposited to your loved one's bank account.

☐ If your loved one is drawing income from retirement accounts as needed, make sure you understand the requirements, fees, and penalties associated with each account and know the balance of each account. Some accounts have penalties for early withdrawals or have minimum withdrawal requirements once your loved one reaches a certain age. This will help you know which accounts to draw money from first to help cover expenses.

☐ If you are named as the representative payee for your loved one's Social Security benefits, you may find it easier to file their annual financial report if you keep the SS funds in a separate account. Use these funds for paying medical bills, mortgage or rent, food, and other necessary expenses, and keep track of each transaction. If you do not need to spend all of this money on necessary expenses each month, save the remainder in an interest-bearing savings account. Do not spend this money on frivolous purchases.

☐ Arrange to have important bills paid automatically each month or mailed directly to you.

☐ Cancel unnecessary credit cards, especially store-specific credit cards. However, before you cancel them, be sure to redeem any points they have gained through the credit card's rewards program. Once you cancel the cards, the rewards are lost forever.

☐ If your loved one needs a credit card, allow them to have one credit card with a low spending limit so they do not overspend on irrational purchases. Alternatively, you could provide them with a reloadable pre-paid card for making purchases and give them a reasonable stipend on the card each month. This money should come from their personal savings or investments, not from government income.

☐ Use a single credit card or ATM/bank card to purchase needed items for your loved one. This credit card should be separate from the account that your loved one has for spending so it can have a higher limit if desired.

☐ If your loved one has multiple bank accounts, retirement accounts, or investments with multiple institutions, consider consolidating them as much as possible. For example, they should have one checking and savings account for personal funds, one checking and savings account for Social Security funds, one pre-paid bank card for your loved one, one credit card for the financial manager, and one institution that handles retirement accounts and investments. If you can manage to have all of these accounts through one institution, that will simplify your life even more.

☐ If your loved one has possessions that require insurance, such as a car or boat, and they are no longer able to use those possessions, consider selling them and canceling the insurance. This helps save money, reduces the number of bills you have to manage, and helps prevent your loved one from participating in unsafe activities.

Tax Benefits for Caregivers

Sometimes it is more convenient to pay for care out of your own pocket rather than using your loved one's funds to cover all costs. The Internal Revenue Service (IRS) offers some tax benefits for situations like these, but only if your loved one is considered your qualifying relative or dependent for tax purposes. The following checklists can serve as a guide to claiming your loved one as a qualifying relative, but please consult an accountant when completing your taxes.

Checklist: Basics about claiming your loved one as a qualifying relative

☐ To claim your loved one as a qualifying relative, they must pass four tests: Not a qualifying child test, Member of household or relationship test, Support test, and Gross income test.

☐ To pass the Not a qualifying child test, your loved one cannot be your qualifying child or the qualifying child of any other taxpayer. Assuming your loved one is not your child, your loved one should pass this test easily. If your loved one is your child, they will have to be claimed as a qualifying child, not a qualifying relative.

☐ To pass the Member of household or relationship test, your loved one must either live with you all year as a member of your household or be related to you in some way, such as a child, sibling, parent or grandparent, niece or nephew, aunt or uncle, or in-law.

☐ To pass the Support test, you must pay for more than half of your loved one's total support during the year. When calculating the extent of your support, be sure to include the fair market value of any space your loved one occupies in your house as well as the cost of bills, utilities, and food. Your loved one's total support includes the support they pay from their own funds or income. Therefore, you must pay more support for your loved one than they pay for themselves.

☐ To pass the Gross income test, your loved one must have earned less than the exemption amount for the tax year. For the 2014 tax year, the exemption amount was $3,950, but this amount is subject to change. Current exemption amounts can be located in *IRS Publication 501, Exemptions, Standard Deduction, and Filing Information.*

☐ Tax-exempt Social Security income does not count toward calculation of your loved one's income. However, if your loved one has income from interest or dividends, for example, part of their Social Security income may be taxable. Taxable income from work, pensions, and other sources is always included.

☐ When calculating your loved one's income, be sure to have on hand relevant Social Security, Veterans Administration, pension, investment, and work documents.

☐ Use IRS Form 1040 or Form 1040A to file your income taxes when claiming your loved one as a qualifying relative. When completing the form, you must provide your loved one's name, relationship to you, and Social Security number. Each one of your dependents counts for one exemption, and each exemption reduces your taxable income.

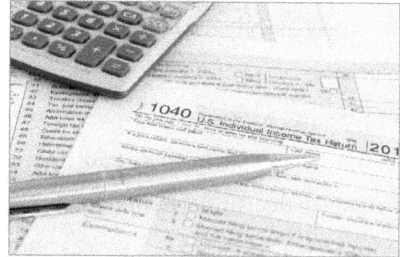

Checklist: Opportunities for tax benefits from the IRS

☐ The major tax benefit of claiming your loved one as a qualifying relative is that you gain an exemption. Each exemption you use reduces your taxable income by several thousand dollars ($3,950 for 2014), thereby reducing your tax bill as well.

☐ If you paid for some of your loved one's medical care, you may be able to deduct those expenses from your taxes. You can claim medical expenses that exceed 10% of your adjusted gross income as itemized deductions (i.e., deductions that exceed the amount of a standard deduction).

☐ If you hired someone to provide care for your dependent loved one while you were working or searching for a job, you may be able to claim the "Child and Dependent Care Credit" on your federal taxes.

☐ If your loved one is legally your dependent, you may be able to use a workplace flexible spending account (FSA) to pay for their medical and care expenses with pretax dollars.

☐ In addition to federal deductions, you may be eligible for state-level deductions or tax credits.

Money-Saving Strategies

In many family situations, it is not practical or possible to save money on taxes by claiming your loved one as a dependent or qualifying relative. Therefore, it is important to look for other ways to save money in order to maximize the amount you have available to spend on your loved one's care. Saving money now will make financial decisions easier in the future, especially if you are using a large share of your own personal finances to pay for care. No matter which money-saving strategies you choose, you will thank yourself later for the money you save.

Checklist: Strategies for saving money

☐ **Food and home care supplies.** Take advantage of sales and stock up on non-perishable items that you or your loved one uses frequently. Avoid purchasing items that you may not use or that may go bad before you use them. Use coupons and buy in bulk and online when it makes sense. If you plan to use coupons, only use the coupon if it is something you would normally buy. If you use a coupon to buy something you would not normally purchase, then you are not saving money.

☐ **Clothing and household items.** Consider shopping at a goodwill or thrift store for clothing and other needed household items. You can often find items in good condition for a cheap price by being willing to shop at secondhand stores.

☐ **Household expenses.** Review cable and telephone services to make sure your loved one is ordering the best plans for their situation. Make sure that appropriate energy-saving strategies are being employed. Many cable and phone companies provide deals for customers who renew services, but you only get the discount if you call in and request it.

- ☐ **Safety.** An ounce of prevention is worth a pound of cure. Upgrade the safety of your loved one's bathroom by installing a few inexpensive items such as toilet or shower rails and non-slip rugs. In addition, purchase other safety equipment as appropriate, such as a walker or bedrails. Many home modifications will help your loved one remain safe and avoid injury, thus saving money on medical bills. For a complete discussion on Alzheimer's disease and safety, see *Home Safety Checklist Guide and Caregiver Resources for Medication Safety, Driving, and Wandering.*

- ☐ **Insurance coverage.** If your loved one is not eligible for Medicare or Medicaid, contact your employer to see whether they might be eligible as a dependent under your health insurance policy. Alternatively, check whether they can get coverage through a group plan offered by a professional organization. For non-medical insurance such as home insurance or car insurance, shop around to multiple insurance agencies to make sure you are getting the best deal.

- ☐ **Prescription drugs.** Look into prescription programs available in your area by visiting the National Council on Aging's BenefitsCheckUp website. Talk with your loved one's doctor about using generic prescriptions rather than brand-name drugs to save money. Many national retailers, such as Target and Walmart, as well as many regional supermarkets and pharmacies, offer certain generic drugs at vastly discounted rates. In addition, some pharmacies, such as Walgreens, offer a Prescription Savings Club for individuals with inadequate prescription drug insurance.

- ☐ **AARP.** The AARP offers discounts, advocacy information, and access to community resources. Membership costs only $16 a year.

- ☐ **Certified Nursing Assistant (CNA) training.** If your loved one lives with you, you can save a great deal of money on unskilled nursing care services by providing care yourself. Becoming licensed typically takes around six weeks, and you can learn how to perform many personal care functions efficiently and safely.

☐ **Service exchange.** If you are able to network with other people in your area who are experiencing similar situations, you may be able to share the load. For example, if a friend also has a loved one with Alzheimer's disease, you might be able to take turns looking after them. Your loved ones may enjoy spending time together, and if their care is simple, one of you could easily take care of both of them for an afternoon.

☐ **Church communities.** Church communities frequently offer charitable and respite care services for members and their loved ones.

Each family has different needs and different resources available, so take some time to investigate the resources in your area to find ways to save money. Saving money on staples such as food and clothing as well as specialty items such as safety modifications or respite care can make a major difference in an already tight budget.

How to Avoid Scams

Even if you take some measure of control over your loved one's finances, Alzheimer's disease still leaves your loved one vulnerable to making poor financial decisions that may cost thousands of dollars. Such decisions are often the result of scams that prey on elderly and mentally compromised individuals. Fraudsters target these individuals because they usually have investments, a lifetime of savings, equity in their homes, and an inability to recognize scams. To learn more about common financial scams that may target your loved one, read the checklist below. Note that some of these scams may come in several forms. For example, similar types of fraud may be perpetrated via mail or over the phone.

Checklist: Common types of financial scams

Mail, e-mail, and Internet scams

☐ Fake companies sell counterfeit drugs or fake "anti-aging" products online for a "special deal."

☐ Someone sends an e-mail stating that they have a fortune they are trying to get out of a corrupt country, and they need your loved one's help to do it. The e-mail states that if your loved one sends a small amount of money to help transfer the fortune, they will receive a large sum of money when the funds become available.

☐ A supposed government organization states that your loved one may have claim to millions of dollars if they fill out a tax form and send in a small fee.

☐ A fake charity sends a letter asking for donations. Frequently, the fake charity uses a logo similar to a real charity so that your loved one thinks they are donating to a charity they trust.

☐ A fraudster sends a letter from what appears to be a legitimate company and asks your loved one to verify their personal information.

☐ A scammer takes bank information from a check and uses that information to make an online withdrawal from your loved one's account.

☐ Your loved one gets a check in the mail that seems like free money. However, the check's fine print states that by depositing the funds, your loved one will be enrolled in a program that charges a monthly fee. Many times, these checks bounce, so your loved one doesn't get any money but is still enrolled in the program.

☐ Your loved one is sent a form to renew a subscription for a magazine they don't currently receive and still won't receive after the renewal.

☐ Someone sends a letter stating that your loved one has won a sweepstakes or lottery, but they need to fill out and return a card with banking information so the money can be deposited into their account. A response to just one of these letters usually precipitates hundreds of similar letters and phone calls.

Dear STEVE D WILLIAMS,

    Attention Please! You need to follow the requested instructions herein as relative to Award Opportunity #7824C for $1,000,000.00 (One Million Dollars) announced by direct letter to you from the AWARD NOTIFICATION COMMISSION corporate headquarters.

    This is an affirmed letter, STEVE D WILLIAMS! Please note that this CONFIRMED opportunity to win and receive the Award is subject to your record of entry validation and completion of the SUBMISSION DOCUMENT (parts A and B on the accompanying page) for your return without delay.

    It is our pleasure to formally inform you of this by private letter, and according to the terms and conditions herein, if you have and return the pre-selected winning number before the deadline as REQUIRED for formal review and authenticity, the payment terms will be yours to select from options #1 and #2 below with no taxes withheld:

    PAYMENT OPTION #1: $33,334.00 ANNUALLY FOR 30 YEARS (TOTAL $1,000,000.00).
    PAYMENT OPTION #2: A SINGLE, LUMP-SUM CERTIFIED CHECK FOR $528,000.00.

    Important: ANC corporate services request your response within 10 DAYS from the date you receive this letter. PLEASE DO NOT DELAY!!

    Subsequent to this, formal mailing arrangements were made by the ANC organization to offer others a chance to win big money. As a result of these ongoing operations, our president has respectfully introduced the following Premium Offer: Genuine "White Fire" Opal pendant. This dazzling Opal pendant is accented with brilliant round Genuine Diamonds & Cubic Zirconia and set on a lovely 18" 14K Gold electroplated chain.

    Kindly note that you must enclose the Amount Due of $54.99 if securing this Premium Offer delivery when completing your SUBMISSION DOCUMENT for return to our offices.

    FINALLY: The only way you can forfeit your opportunity to WIN and receive the Award of *** $1,000,000.00 *** is by not submitting your entry in time, by mail. As such, PLEASE DO NOT DELAY. If determined WINNER, the optional payment choice is definitely the yours for $33,334.00 CASH every year for 30 consecutive years ($1,000,000.00 TOTAL) or a generous lump-sum single payment of $528,000.00.

    Accordingly, our fondest wishes prevail for you now and always. Please be prompt with your reply!

                    Sincerely,

                   Jefferson P. Williams
                   Prize Officer, AWARD NOTIFICATION COMMISSION

☐ A company mails crossword puzzles to your loved one with the promise that completing the puzzles correctly and returning them with $10 or $15 will enter the person in a lottery with huge prizes. The company might appeal to the victim's vanity by complimenting their intelligence.

Phone scams

☐ A medical equipment company offers free equipment in exchange for your loved one's Medicaid number. Once the company has that number, they use it to bill Medicaid for fraudulent charges.

☐ A telemarketer calls and states that your loved one has won a prize, sweepstakes, or lottery. The only catch is that your loved one has to provide credit card or bank account information to collect the money. These calls usually originate from a Jamaican area code (876), even if the calls are not actually placed from Jamaica.

☐ Someone calls pretending to be a loved one in trouble and asks for money right away.

☐ Someone calls pretending to be a government agency—maybe Medicaid—and asks your loved one to verify personal information such as bank account number, Social Security number, or Medicaid or Medicare claim numbers.

☐ Someone calls pretending to be from your loved one's credit card company and says that they want to ask about potentially suspicious charges as a way of extracting your loved one's credit card number.

☐ After a natural disaster, someone pretending to be from a well-known crisis charity (like the Red Cross) calls your loved one to ask for "donations."

☐ Someone calls stating that an assassination contract has been placed on your loved one, but if they pay a large fee, the contract will be cancelled.

☐ A fake utility service calls your loved one and says their electricity or gas is going to be turned off because of unpaid bills. The con artists may even send someone to your loved one's door to collect payment.

In-person scams

☐ A salesman tells your loved one that an amazing deal—usually an investment of some sort—is only good today, so they must make a decision immediately.

☐ A repairman comes to the door, stating that he was driving by and noticed that your loved one's roof or gutters needed fixing. The fraudulent handyman might ask for payment up front and then never complete the work, or he may simply continue finding things that need to be "repaired." Disreputable local businesses sometimes attempt similar schemes.

☐ Your loved one is offered a free lunch in exchange for attending a seminar. While at the seminar, they are pressured into purchasing poor or bogus investments. These investments often advertise "guaranteed" returns.

☐ A criminal tries to sell your loved one a home security inspection in order to gain access to their residence and case it for a burglary.

Family scams

☐ Family members or friends who have access to your loved one's accounts use that access to steal money.

☐ Family members or friends who previously had little contact with your loved one suddenly show up and want to help "manage" your loved one's finances.

☐ A family member or friend goes with your loved one to the bank to supervise the withdrawal of a large sum of money.

To ensure cooperation, fraudsters may threaten your loved one or a family member with physical harm. They may also tell your loved one that they will be placed in a nursing home and lose their independence should any family members learn about the fraud. In the face of these threats, your loved one may hide or deny that any scams have taken place. If your loved one is hiding their actions, how can you determine whether they have been scammed? The checklist below describes some common evidence of scams.

Checklist: How to identify whether your loved one is a target of scams

☐ Your loved one gets numerous phone calls from a Jamaican area code.

☐ Your loved one tries to wire large sums of money, especially to other countries.

☐ Your loved one's junk mail volume increases suddenly.

☐ Your loved one's bank accounts are missing large sums of money.

☐ Your loved one adds names you don't recognize to their bank accounts.

☐ Your loved one no longer receives bank statements.

☐ Your loved one suddenly has several unpaid bills.

☐ Your loved one wants to use the ATM frequently.

☐ Your loved one keeps large amounts of cash at home.

☐ Your loved one purchases unnecessary services or repairs.

☐ Your loved one changes their will or living trust frequently.

☐ Your loved one seems afraid of a specific friend or family member.

☐ Your loved one has a hard time explaining how they spent money.

☐ Your loved one has a new friend that you've never met before.

If your loved one seems to be especially susceptible to scams, you can take several steps to help your loved one avoid scams. These steps may take some time and a small investment, but they will save you a lot of headache in the future.

Checklist: How to protect your loved one from scams

Monitoring finances

☐ Obtain power of attorney over your loved one's finances, if reasonable. If you are not available be your loved one's power of attorney, find someone who can assume power of attorney and monitor your loved one's finances for you.

☐ Set up an auto-pay system for your loved one's monthly bills. That way, when fake utility companies say that a bill hasn't been paid, you can explain to your loved one that all bills are paid automatically.

☐ Frequently monitor your loved one's bills and bank statements to detect scams early.

☐ Take away your loved one's checkbook, and sit down each week to pay legitimate bills.

☐ If you have power of attorney over finances, create an account from which your loved one can access a small amount of money each week or month. Your loved one can use this money however they see fit. Keep all other financial resources in separate accounts that your loved one has no control over. Use the money in these accounts to pay bills and other legitimate expenses.

☐ For individuals who feel it is important to have cash on hand, provide several small bills rather than one large bill.

☐ Close accounts that have been scammed and open new accounts.

☐ Alert the bank and credit card company that your loved one is not competent and is being preyed on by scammers.

☐ Opt out of future credit card and other offers by calling the Opt-In/Opt-Out Request Line at (888) 567-8688.

☐ If your loved one wants to donate to a worthy cause, research the cause together and submit the donation through verified channels.

☐ Have your loved one set up a trust. Money in trusts is carefully monitored and difficult to access.

Preventing phone scams

☐ Change your loved one's phone number to an unlisted number. Tell your loved one not to give out the new number, or don't tell it to them in the first place.

☐ Post a note next to the phone reminding your loved one never to give out personal information over the phone.

☐ Turn off the ringers on your loved one's phone. Set the answering machine to pick up on the first ring.

☐ Put anonymous call blocking on your loved one's phone so that all parties who are calling have to identify themselves.

☐ Get a phone with no caller ID so your loved one cannot call back numbers from missed calls.

☐ Consider installing a device on your loved one's telephone that prevents computer-generated calls from getting through.

☐ Block specific incoming phone numbers that you know are from scammers.

☐ Install a call blocker with "whitelist" capabilities. This device will block all calls except those from approved phone numbers already entered into the system. When setting up the blocker, only allow calls from phone numbers of trusted individuals, such as loved ones, doctor's offices, the bank, etc.

☐ Monitor your loved one's phone calls online. If you notice your loved one is receiving phone calls from a Jamaican area code (876), change their number yet again.

☐ Place your loved one's number on the Do Not Call registry either online or by calling 1-888-382-1222.

Preventing mail scams

☐ Purchase a locking mailbox for the street. Ask the mail carrier to never hand deliver any mail to your loved one but to always put it in the locked box.

☐ Purchase a P.O. Box and route all your loved one's mail through this box. Check the P.O. Box daily and hand deliver only legitimate mail.

☐ Authorize the post office to stop delivering third-class mail.

☐ Shred all documents such as scam letters and credit card applications rather than just throwing them in the trash. Some individuals with Alzheimer's disease will go through the trash, find the letters, fill them out, and mail them in.

☐ Reduce junk mail by printing and filling out an official form and submitting it to the following service. Make sure to include all spellings and variations of your loved one's name:

> DMAchoice
> Direct Marketing Association
> P.O. Box 643
> Carmel, NY 10512
> https://www.dmachoice.org/register.php

- [ ] Send an e-mail to the scammers telling them to take your loved one's name off their list, and ask them to send one reply e-mail indicating they will do this. If they won't, tell them that you will refer them to your lawyer for litigation and potential prosecution. Include your attorney's contact information in the e-mail.

Preventing in-person scams

- [ ] Post a "no solicitors" sign on your loved one's front door. If a solicitor comes to your loved one's door, immediately report them to the police so the police can scan the neighborhood and talk to them.

- [ ] Write a letter to your loved one explaining that the house does not need to be repaired, they do not need new insurance policies or investments, and they do not need other services that you have encountered in scams in your area. Post the reminder next to your loved one's door and phone.

- [ ] Call 911 if your loved one is in immediate danger from an in-person scammer.

Teaching your loved one about scams

- [ ] Teach your loved one to discuss all financial decisions with you before committing. This will help your loved one avoid situations in which they have to say "no."

- [ ] Remind your loved one that if a deal sounds too good to be true, it usually is.

- [ ] Talk to your loved one about why a particular letter or phone call is a scam (e.g., you can't win a contest you didn't enter, you never have to pay to collect winnings from a real sweepstakes, and so on).

- [ ] Teach your loved one that if someone pressures you to make a decision and pay immediately, it is a scam. Any legitimate business person would give your loved one time to make the right decision.

- [ ] Remind your loved one that they taught you to always be wary of strangers.

- [ ] Play devil's advocate. Ask your loved one whether you can get involved with the scam as well. Sometimes their need to protect you from the scam will help them realize that they are being scammed.

- ☐ Spend time with your loved one. Many elderly individuals talk to scammers because con artists pretend to care, and many elderly people just want someone to talk to.

- ☐ Plan an event for family and friends that your loved one will pay for. Giving your loved one a reason to save money will help them not spend it on scams.

What to do if your loved one has been scammed

- ☐ Contact a local, state, or federal agency if your loved one has been contacted by scammers.

- ☐ Tell your loved one that the authorities are looking for these scammers, so they can provide valuable help if they give the authorities information about the scam.

- ☐ Report suspected cases of fraud to the National Consumer League's Fraud Center, or call the Federal Trade Commission's Consumer Response Center at (877) 382-4357. Mail-in complaints can be sent to:

  > NCL's Fraud.org
  > c/o National Consumers League
  > 1701 K Street NW, Suite 1200
  > Washington, DC 20006

- ☐ Report suspected cases of fraud to your state's attorney general.

- ☐ Don't give up! Scammers are persistent, so you may need to try several of these tactics multiple times, especially if the scammers have already received some money from your loved one.

Another important step that you can take to protect your loved one is to purchase identity theft protection. Identity theft protection helps monitor your loved one's Social Security number, credit card numbers, address, birth date, and other information to detect potential identity theft. The company then sends an alert to your loved one if identity theft is detected or suspected. Some companies will even help you with the recovery processes, depending on the type of protection provided. Some policies help reimburse your loved one's losses, whereas others reimburse you for money spent to complete the identity recovery. Each identity theft protection company has different sites that they monitor, different costs for services, different reports provided, and different recovery services provided, so you will need to do some research to determine which company is best for your situation. Most companies charge between $8 and $28 per month, depending on the level of services. Some companies that provide identity theft protection are listed below. Note that this is not a comprehensive list. Many banks, agencies, and major insurance companies also provide identity theft protection plans.

Checklist: Companies that offer identity theft protection

- ☐ LifeLock

- ☐ LegalShield IDShield

- ☐ Identity Guard

- ☐ IdentityForce

- ☐ ID Watchdog

- ☐ InfoArmor

- ☐ PrivacyGuard

- ☐ IdentitySecure

Checklist: Potential services provided by identity theft protection companies

- ☐ Sends alerts if identity theft is suspected

- ☐ Helps cancel or replace credit cards, driver's licenses, and other cards if your loved one's wallet is lost or stolen; may also provide access to emergency funds until their accounts can be restored

- ☐ Verifies change of address requests, especially for financial information that may have been diverted by identity thieves

- ☐ Removes your loved one's name from pre-approved credit card mailing lists

- ☐ Monitors credit card, checking, and savings accounts for cash withdrawals, balance transfers, and large purchases

- [ ] Notifies you if a large-scale identity breach occurs, even if it doesn't end up affecting your loved one's identity

- [ ] Scans for fraudulent activity associated with your loved one's Social Security number, including publishing of their personal information in non-secure locations online

- [ ] Monitors retirement and investment accounts for fraudulent withdrawals

- [ ] Monitors credit checks for fraudulent activity; credit checks are often performed if someone applies for a new credit card, bank account, cell phone account, mortgage, or other loans

- [ ] Monitors new application activity for bank accounts opened in your loved one's name

- [ ] Monitors your loved one's accounts for the addition of new account holders

- [ ] Monitors file sharing sites for fraudulent use of your loved one's identity

- [ ] Monitors criminal/black market websites for your loved one's data

- [ ] Scans court records for your loved one's data to prevent false convictions

- [ ] Monitors for changes to your loved one's publicly available information

- [ ] Helps restore your loved one's identity if identity theft occurs; some companies perform the restoration themselves, and some companies will guide you through the steps to restore your loved one's identity; some companies will spend up to $1 million for these activities, including legal fees, accountant fees, and investigative fees

- [ ] Provides access to three free annual credit reports

- [ ] Provides antivirus, anti-spyware, and firewall software for your loved one's computer

Identity theft protection plans do not prevent your loved one's identity from getting stolen. Instead, you will be notified more quickly that fraudulent activity has taken place so that you can remedy the situation before it gets out of control. Many people make the mistake of buying identity theft protection and then feeling like they are no longer vulnerable to scams or identity theft. Even with identity theft protection, your loved one still needs to be careful not to give out personal information to strangers. If your loved one is a victim of identity theft, you should report the theft to the Federal Trade Commission. They will help you through the steps needed to recover from identity theft, even if you don't have identity theft protection.

Conclusion

Dealing with the financial needs and responsibilities of an individual with Alzheimer's disease can be overwhelming at times. Understanding your loved one's insurance needs and policies, their personal finances, and the resources available to them will require that you spend a lot of time talking about finances with your loved one and researching their financial options. As their disease progresses, your loved one will become increasingly unable to participate in these conversations, so you should start early. If you strive to understand your loved one's financial resources early in the course of the disease, you will have fewer barriers to providing good care when your loved one needs assistance with everyday living activities such as eating, bathing, and toileting.

ABOUT THE AUTHORS

Laura Town

Laura Town has authored numerous publications of special interest to the aging population. She has expertise in the field of finance as a co-author on *Finance: Foundations of Financial Institutions and Management*, published by John Wiley and Sons, and she has contributed to several online nursing courses and texts. She has also written for the American Medical Writers Association, and her work has been published by the American Society of Journalists and Authors. As an editor, Laura has worked with Pearson Education, Prentice Hall, McGraw-Hill Higher Education, John Wiley and Sons, and the University of Pennsylvania to create both on-ground and online courses and texts. She is currently the President of the Indiana chapter of the American Medical Writers Association.

Karen Kassel

Karen Kassel received her Ph.D. in pharmacology from the Department of Pharmacology and Experimental Neurosciences at the University of Nebraska Medical Center in Omaha, where she was the recipient of an American Heart Association fellowship and several regional and national awards for her research on G protein-coupled receptor signaling in airways. She then pursued post-doctoral research projects at the University of North Carolina–Chapel Hill and the University of Kansas Medical Center, again receiving fellowships from the PhRMA Foundation and the American Heart Association, respectively. She has published research in the *American Journal of Pathology*, *Journal of Biological Chemistry*, and *Journal of Pharmacology and Experimental Therapeutics*. In 2012, Karen joined the editorial staff at WilliamsTown Communications, an editing firm that specializes in educational products for undergraduate- and graduate-level students. At WTC, Karen specializes in producing educational products related to the sciences and healthcare. In addition, Karen is board-certified for editing life sciences (BELS-certified).

Sam Clapp

Sam Clapp earned a bachelor's degree in English from Washington University in St. Louis. He has been an editor and writer for WilliamsTown Communications since 2012. Sam has served as a writer for textbook projects, articles, and web copy and as an instructional designer for online courses. As an editor, he has contributed to management, nursing, and technology books.

A NOTE FROM THE AUTHORS

Thank you for purchasing our book! Worldwide, over 40 million people suffer from Alzheimer's disease, and that number is expected to increase significantly within the next 15 years. In the United States, five million people have the disease, and that is expected to triple by the year 2050.

Despite these large numbers, you may feel alone. I (Laura) know that when I started caring for my father, who had early-onset Alzheimer's disease, I felt alone. Although my father has passed away, I am haunted by what he suffered and how difficult it was to care for him. However, now I know that there are people, resources, and organizations that can help others going through this same struggle.

We recognize that caregivers have emotional, physical, and financial challenges. We hope that the information in the *Alzheimer's Roadmap* series will ease some of your stress. The topics discussed in this book will help you prepare for that inevitable day when your loved one is no longer able to make their own decisions about healthcare and finances. In addition, we have included resources at the end of each book to provide more information to help you through this process.

If you have any questions for us, feel free to post them on Laura Town's Amazon Author Central page or reach out to either author via Twitter: @laurawtown and @KarenKassel1. We would appreciate it if you would take the time to review our book on Amazon, as our book's visibility on Amazon depends on reviews.

More Titles from Laura Town and Karen Kassel

☐ *Long-Term Care Insurance, Power of Attorney, Wealth Management, and Other First Steps*

☐ *Dementia, Alzheimer's Disease Stages, Treatments, and Other Medical Considerations*

☐ *Advance Directives, Durable Power of Attorney, Wills, and Other Legal Considerations*

☐ *Home Safety Checklist Guide and Caregiver Resources for Medication Safety, Driving, and Wandering*

☐ *Home Care, Long-Term Care, Memory Care Units, and Other Living Arrangements*

☐ *Caregiver Resources for Helping with Activities of Daily Living*

☐ *Nutrition for Brain Health: Fighting Dementia*

☐ *Caregiver Resources: From Independence to a Memory Care Unit*

(This book combines information from *Home Safety Checklist Guide and Caregiver Resources for Medication Safety, Driving, and Wandering* and information from *Home Care, Long-Term Care, Memory Care Units, and Other Living Arrangements*.)

RESOURCES

Insurance Resources

Affordable Care Act Marketplace

Website: http://www.healthcare.gov/get-coverage/

*Provides enrollment and information resources for the Health Insurance Marketplace

Medicare Resources

Centers for Medicare and Medicaid Services

7500 Security Boulevard

Baltimore, MD 21244

Phone: 877-267-2323

General information: http://www.medicare.gov/

Eligibility and premium calculator: http://www.medicare.gov/eligibilitypremiumcalc/

Online application: https://secure.ssa.gov/iClaim/rib

Initial Enrollment Questionnaire: https://www.mymedicare.gov/

Health insurance counseling from SHIP: https://www.shiptacenter.org/

Medicare plan finder: https://www.medicare.gov/find-a-plan/questions/home.aspx

Medigap plans: https://www.medicare.gov/find-a-plan/questions/medigap-home.aspx?AspxAutoDetectCookieSupport=1

Medicare Savings Program: http://www.medicare.gov/contacts/#resources/msps

Medicaid Resources

General information: http://medicaid.gov/

Medicaid screener: https://www.healthcare.gov/screener/

Locate state Medicaid resources: http://www.medicaid.gov/medicaid-chip-program-information/by-state/by-state.html

Federal poverty level charts: http://www.medicaid.gov/medicaid-chip-program-information/by-topics/eligibility/downloads/2015-federal-poverty-level-charts.pdf

PACE service areas: http://www.npaonline.org/custom/programsearch.asp?id=209

Children's Health Insurance Program: https://www.healthcare.gov/medicaid-chip/childrens-health-insurance-program/

Personal Finances Resources

Thrift Savings Plans: https://www.tsp.gov/index.shtml

IRA minimum distribution worksheet: http://www.irs.gov/pub/irs-tege/uniform_rmd_wksht.pdf

Social Security Resources

Phone: 1-800-772-1213 (TTY 1-800-325-0778)
General information: https://secure.ssa.gov/i1020/start
Social Security retirement estimator: http://www.ssa.gov/retire/estimator.html
Apply for Social Security benefits: https://secure.ssa.gov/iClaim/rib
Locate local Social Security office: https://secure.ssa.gov/ICON/main.jsp
Adult disability checklist: http://www.ssa.gov/hlp/radr/10/ovw001-checklist.pdf
Apply for Social Security disability: https://secure.ssa.gov/iClaim/dib
Medical release form: http://www.socialsecurity.gov/forms/ssa-827.pdf
Supplemental Security Income screening: http://ssabest.benefits.gov/

Military Resources

U.S. Department of Veterans Affairs

810 Vermont Avenue, NW
Washington DC 20420
Phone: 1-800-827-1000
TRICARE: http://www.tricare.mil/
Find a local VA office:
http://www.va.gov/directory/guide/division.asp?dnum=3&isFlash=0
VA website: http://www.va.gov/

Government Resources

SNAP eligibility: http://www.snap-step1.usda.gov/fns/
Administration on Aging: http://www.aoa.acl.gov/
Government benefits: http://www.benefits.gov/
National Council on Aging: http://www.ncoa.org; http://www.benefitscheckup.org

Information Resources

Alzheimer's Association

225 N. Michigan Avenue, Floor 17
Chicago, IL 60601-7633
Phone: 800-272-3900
Fax: 866-699-1246
E-mail: info@alz.org
Website: http://www.alz.org

Alzheimer's Foundation of America
322 Eighth Avenue, 7th floor
New York, NY 10001
Phone: 866-232-8484
Fax: 646-638-1546
Website: http://www.alzfdn.org

American Association of Retired Persons
Website: http://aarp.org

Fisher Center for Alzheimer's Research Foundation
110 E 42nd Street, 16th Floor
New York, NY 10017
Phone: 1-800-259-4636
Fax: 1-212-915-1319
E-mail: info@alzinfo.org
Website: http://www.alzinfo.org

Alzheimer's Roadmap series

- *Long-Term Care Insurance, Power of Attorney, Wealth Management, and Other First Steps*

- *Dementia, Alzheimer's Disease Stages, Treatment Options, and Other Medical Considerations*

- *Advance Directives, Durable Power of Attorney, Wills, and Other Legal Considerations*

- *Home Safety Checklist Guide and Caregiver Resources for Medication Safety, Driving, and Wandering*

- *Home Care, Long-term Care, Memory Care Units, and Other Living Arrangements*

- *Caregiver Resources for Helping with Activities of Daily Living*

- *Nutrition for Brain Health: Fighting Dementia*

- *Caregiver Resources: From Independence to a Memory Care Unit*

  (This book combines information from *Home Safety Checklist Guide and Caregiver Resources for Medication Safety, Driving, and Wandering* and information from *Home Care, Long-Term Care, Memory Care Units, and Other Living Arrangements*.)

REFERENCE LIST

AARP. (2015). Retrieved from http://www.aarp.org/

Alzheimer's Association. (2014). Retrieved from http://www.alz.org/

Alzheimers.gov. (n.d.). How to pay and plan ahead. Retrieved from
http://www.alzheimers.gov/paying.html

Alzheimer's Society. (2014). Top tips for managing money and preventing financial
abuse. Retrieved from http://www.alzheimers.org.uk/site/scripts/
documents_info.php?documentID=1772

Anderson, J. (2014). Top 10 senior scams and how to avoid them. *A Place for Mom.*
Retrieved from http://www.aplaceformom.com/blog/3-8-14-senior-scams-
how-to-avoid/

Barron Ross. (2014). Medicare and Medicaid. Retrieved from
http://www.barronross.com/long-term-care/medicare-and-medicaid/

BenefitsCheckUp. (n.d.). Retrieved from http://www.benefitscheckup.org

Benefits.gov. (2014). Retrieved from http://www.govbenefits.gov

Block, S. (2012). Claiming an adult child as a dependent on your taxes. *USA Today.*
Retrieved from http://usatoday30.usatoday.com/money/perfi/columnist/
block/story/2012-01-30/claiming-adult-children-as-dependents-taxes/
52890686/1

Boerger, G. H. (2012). Estate planning and my house (or my parents' house): What
are the options? Retrieved from http://boergerlaw.com/archives/366

Caring.com. (2014). How do we protect my grandfather from scams? Retrieved
from http://www.caring.com/questions/alzheimers-and-money-scams

Center for Medicare Advocacy. (n.d.). Medicare coverage for people with
disabilities. Retrieved from http://www.medicareadvocacy.org/medicare-
info/medicare-coverage-for-people-with-disabilities/

Center for Medicare and Medicaid Services. (2014). Dual eligible beneficiaries under
the Medicare and Medicaid Programs. Retrieved from http://www.cms.gov/
Outreach-and-Education/Medicare-Learning-Network-MLN/MLNProducts/
downloads/Medicare_Beneficiaries_Dual_Eligibles_At_a_Glance.pdf

Cleaver, J. (2014). How to choose between a revocable and irrevocable trust. Retrieved from http://money.usnews.com/money/personal-finance/mutual-funds/articles/2014/06/19/how-to-choose-between-a-revocable-and-irrevocable-trust

CNN Money. (2014). Ultimate guide to retirement. Retrieved from http://money.cnn.com/retirement/guide/annuities_basics.moneymag/

Cooper, R. (2013). Golden years can be a gold mine for scammers who target our seniors. *Alzheimers North Carolina, Inc.* Retrieved from http://www.alznc.org/index.php/alzheimers-legal-financial-information/73-protecting-seniors-from-scams

Defense Health Agency. (2015). http://www.tricare.mil/

ElderLawAnswers. (2014). Protecting your house from Medicaid estate recovery. Retrieved from http://www.elderlawanswers.com/protecting-your-house-from-medicaid-estate-recovery-12155

Elliott, K. R., & Moore, J. H., Jr. (2000). Cash balance pension plans: The new wave. *Compensation and Working Conditions, Summer,* 3–11.

FDIC. (2014). For seniors: Fifteen quick tips for protecting your finances. Retrieved from https://www.fdic.gov/consumers/consumer/news/cnsum13/quicktips.html

Healthcare.gov. (2014). Apply for Medicaid and CHIP. Retrieved from https://www.healthcare.gov/coverage-outside-open-enrollment/medicaid-chip/

Hellsell Fetterman. (2015). Irrevocable trusts. Retrieved from http://www.helsell.com/faq/irrevocable-trusts/

Hungelmann, J. (2014). Can I borrow from my life insurance policy? *Bankrate.* Retrieved from http://www.bankrate.com/finance/insurance/borrow-from-life-insurance-policy.aspx

Iam National Pension Fund. (2014). Apply for pension benefits. Retrieved from http://mypension.iamnpf.org/national-pension-plan/apply-for-pension-benefits.aspx

Identity Guard. (2015). Retrieved from http://www.identityguard.com/

Illinois Department of Healthcare and Family Services. (2015). HFS 591SP Medicaid Spenddown. Retrieved from http://www2.illinois.gov/hfs/MedicalPrograms/Brochures/Pages/HFS591SP.aspx

Internal Revenue Service. (2014). Retrieved from http://www.irs.gov/

Intuit TurboTax. (2014). Retrieved from https://turbotax.intuit.com/

Landen, R. (2014). Pattern of problems with the Veterans Affairs healthcare system. *Modern Healthcare*. Retrieved from http://www.modernhealthcare.com/article/20140507/NEWS/305079939

LifeLock. (2015). Retrieved from https://www.lifelock.com/

Loth, R. (2014). Retirement plans. *Investopedia*. Retrieved from http://www.investopedia.com/university/retirementplans/

Lyman, K. (2015). Are revocable or irrevocable living trusts useful in qualifying for Medicaid? Retrieved from http://www.nolo.com/legal-encyclopedia/are-revocable-irrevocable-living-trusts-useful-qualifying-medicaid.html

Medicaid.gov. (2014). Retrieved from http://www.medicaid.gov/

Medicare.gov. (2015). Retrieved from http://www.medicare.gov/

Military.com. (2015). Retrieved from http://www.military.com/benefits/tricare

Mooney, S. M. (2012). Life estate ownership of real estate. Retrieved from http://www.susanmooney.com/?page_id=530

National Center for Employee Ownership. (2015). ESOP Facts. Retrieved from http://www.esop.org/

National Institute on Aging. (2011). Alzheimer's disease and managing finances. Retrieved from http://www.nia.nih.gov/alzheimers/publication/alzheimers-disease-and-managing-finances

National Reverse Mortgage Lenders Association. (2014). Your guide to reverse mortgages. Retrieved from http://www.reversemortgage.org/

New York State Department of Health. (2010). Medicaid excess income. Retrieved from https://www.health.ny.gov/health_care/medicaid/excess_income.htm

Pabian & Russell, LLC. (2015). Irrevocable asset protection trust. Retrieved from http://www.pabianrussell.com/Elder-Law/irrevocable-asset-protection-trust

Rando, D. (2014). Cashing in your life insurance policy. *Investopedia*. Retrieved from http://www.investopedia.com/articles/pf/08/life-insurance-cash-in.asp

Sherman, F. (n.d.). Should I put my house into an irrevocable trust? Retrieved from http://homeguides.sfgate.com/should-put-house-irrevocable-trust-72197.html

Social Security Administration. (2014). Retrieved from http://www.ssa.gov/

South Dakota Office of the Attorney General. (n.d.). Durable power of attorney. Retrieved from http://atg.sd.gov/Seniors/EstatePlanning/PowerofAttorney.aspx

Thrift Savings Plan. (2015). Contribution limits. Retrieved from https://www.tsp.gov/planparticipation/eligibility/contributionLimits.shtml

United States Department of Defense. (2015). Military compensation. Retrieved from http://militarypay.defense.gov/retirement/

United States Department of Health and Human Services. (2005). Medicaid estate recovery. Retrieved from http://aspe.hhs.gov/daltcp/reports/estaterec.htm

United States Department of Labor. (n.d.). http://www.dol.gov/

United States Department of Veterans Affairs. (2014). Retrieved from http://www.va.gov/

Wells Fargo Advisors. (2014). Wealth transfer and gifting. Retrieved from https://www.wellsfargoadvisors.com/financial-services/estate-planning/gifting-wealth-transfer.htm

www.ingramcontent.com/pod-product-compliance
Lightning Source LLC
Chambersburg PA
CBHW081648270326
41933CB00018B/3386